THE HISTORY FILES

HISTORY'S GREATEST HITS

The first wave of US troops hit the water from their landing craft off Omaha Beach in Normandy, France, on D-Day.

THE HISTORY FILES

HISTORY'S GREATEST HITS

FAMOUS EVENTS WE SHOULD ALL KNOW ABOUT

JOSEPH CUMMINS

PIER 9

CONTENTS

★ THE EARLY MODERN ERA
1500–1900

★ A WORLD AT WAR
1900–1950

★ THE COLD WAR AND BEYOND
1950–2001

INTRODUCTION

A long time ago, people learned history by crouching eagerly at the feet of a storyteller, listening to spoken tales told of great deeds of the past. The nineteenth century English writer William Makepeace Thackeray wrote that such tales were 'heard by the Northmen Vikings, as they lay on their shields on deck; and by the Arabs, couched under the stars in the Syrian plains, when the flocks were gathered in, and the mares were picketed by the tents'.

Later, of course, that changed, and the printed word replaced the spoken. However, history books were often serious, dry and formal, lacking the drama and embellishments of a skilled storyteller — plucked clean of the very detail that might interest and intrigue.

Fortunately, we live in an age where this is no longer true, because the finest story from history is just as surprising and dramatic as the best fictional story. *History's Greatest Hits* is a collection of twenty-two events from the past chosen to fascinate and, hopefully, to teach you about the importance to our lives today of even seemingly remote events.

The danse macabre — *the dance of death — personified people's fear of the Black Death during the Middle Ages.*

Take the Black Death, for instance. This terrible bubonic plague epidemic swept through Europe from 1347 to 1349, killing thirty-five million people — one in out of every three people. This is a dry, although shocking, fact. But what this dry fact does not convey is an understanding of how people at the time responded to the plague. How they called it, not the Black Death (a name made up for it 200 years later), but the much more natural, and somehow more terrible, Big

Death — as in: 'The Big Death is in the next village!' And how some people partied, and some hid, and some people became so obsessed with death that it was all they could think about. Our understanding is further enriched when we learn that, after the plague was over, many people appreciated life a great deal more, got married as soon as they could, and had children.

A little-known fact is that the Black Death killed so many people it actually provided more opportunities for those left behind. The standard of living for farmers and labourers rose — they could get better wages because their services were more in demand. What are we to think of this? Can something good come from something so terrible? It's a great question to ponder, the kind of question that learning about history brings to mind.

Finally — and here is a direct connection to a vanished world — although we can treat most epidemics today with powerful modern drugs, the fear of another Black Death remains inside all of us, which is why we work so hard to keep contagions like the swine flu from spreading. This tiny remnant of fear within our chests is a cast-off spark from the vast conflagration that consumed our fellow human beings so long ago.

One of the reasons we tell stories is to try to clear things up — there's a lot of misinformation, even within families: 'No, your Uncle Harry was not sent to jail for throwing rocks at Grandma's cat, despite what Grandma may have told you.' There's an equal amount of wrong — although generally accepted — information handed down about famous historical events, the sort of information that makes us think we know a lot about what happened when we don't necessarily. Hopefully, *History's Greatest Hits* will help you keep the record straight when it comes to stories like that of the assassination of Julius Caesar (no, he did not say 'Et tu, Brutus') or the storming of the Bastille (political prisoners were not freed — because the prison was empty except for four common criminals and two lunatics). The ability to discern the true story — or to at least take what you read with a grain of salt until further evidence is attained — is a very valuable trait in our current age of instant communication.

Which brings us to our last reason for reading *History's Greatest Hits*. History is not just what happened, it is how it happened. We probably don't absolutely need to know the way the Taino Indians wore their hair when Columbus showed up on their little island in 1492, nor just what a British 'Tommy' thought as he was about to go on the attack at the bloody Battle of the Somme in 1916. Nor do we absolutely need to know that a politician's wife said to President John F. Kennedy, moments before he was assassinated in Texas, 'Mr President, you can't say that Dallas doesn't love you!'

Yet having these images and words in our heads provides us with a much fuller understanding of what occurred because we can see and feel it — and this helps us to remember it too. Melding the oral tradition of storytellers of a much earlier time with the facts that modern historical methods can uncover should give readers the very best of both worlds.

Centuries after the fall of the Roman Empire, an eighteenth century artist depicted two monuments to its past glories — the Colosseum (left) and the Arch of Constantine (right).

THE ANCIENT WORLD

[250 BC–500 AD]

HANNIBAL CROSSES THE ALPS

THE

[218 BC]

★ ★ ★ ★ ★ ★ ★ ★ ★ ★ ★ ★ ★ ★ ★

How one of history's most determined leaders drove an entire army – and a herd of elephants – over Western Europe's highest mountains

In treacherous conditions, Hannibal's men and their elephants wind their way upwards through ever-narrowing gorges and passes.

In the third century BC, the ancient North African kingdom of Carthage fought Rome for control of the Mediterranean basin. The up-and-coming power of Rome lay roughly to its north, across the Mediterranean. This lengthy and bloody conflict— known as the Punic Wars — took three wars and one hundred years to resolve. In the end, Rome was the victor. The once-grand old city of Carthage burned to ashes, its people were sold into slavery, and its very earth was sown with salt, so that nothing could ever grow there again. After this victory, Rome was well on its way to establishing its thousand-year empire, while Carthage became merely an echoing and distant memory. Except, that is, for one man: Hannibal Barca. His extraordinary feat of crossing the Alps with a large army — and a herd of battle elephants — has captured human imaginations for over 2000 years.

It's doubtful whether we would know anything about Hannibal were it not for a Greek-born historian named Polybius. Writing fifty years after the event, he relates one instance of Hannibal's leadership. Standing in the foothills of the Alps, with mountains of indescribable height looming behind him — mountains no army had ever crossed — Hannibal addressed his nervous men: 'What do you think the Alps are? They are nothing more than high mountains … No height is insurmountable to men of determination.'

Hannibal had devised an extraordinary military strategy. Rather than attack Italy by sea, which the Romans with their powerful navy could readily guard against, he would attack from the north, after leading his men through mountains many thought impassable.

★ ★ ★ ★ ★

'I WILL USE FIRE AND STEEL'

The Punic Wars were about territory and wealth. ('Punic' derives from the Latin word *Punicus*, meaning 'Phoenician', as Carthage had begun as a Phoenician colony.) In the third century BC, Carthage, located in modern-day Tunisia, controlled much of the region. This included the islands of Corsica, Sardinia and Sicily, south-eastern Spain, and a good deal of the North African coast to present-day Israel. Rome, on the other hand, had conquered many of the city-states of the Italian Peninsula and wanted to extend its influence into the Mediterranean. The First Punic War began in 264 BC as a battle for control of Sicily and lasted twenty-three years. Carthage lost this battle and turned its attention to building up an empire in Spain. But the Romans weren't about to let that happen either.

In 221 BC, Hannibal Barca, the twenty-five-year-old son of a legendary commander, took control of Carthaginian forces in Spain after his father was killed fighting the local tribes. He immediately began an aggressive campaign against some of the wild tribes to the north. Defying the Romans he besieged the city of Saguntum (now Sagunto), and in 218 BC the city fell to the Carthaginians in an orgy of slaughter. Diplomatic relations between Carthage and Rome were then broken off and the Second Punic War commenced.

It was said that when he was still a child Hannibal had sworn an oath that 'as soon as age will permit … I will use fire and steel to resolve the destiny of Rome'. Whatever it took now, Hannibal was not about to allow Carthage to lose another war to Rome, for he knew that it would mean the utter destruction of his homeland. Soon, he began to put his plan for an overland attack on Italy into motion.

WHICH WAY TO ITALY?

The question that has plagued scholars for generations is: which way did Hannibal go? Most historians have Hannibal following the Rhône north to where it joins with the eastward-flowing Isère River. This would have taken him to one of numerous transverse valleys which he might have followed generally south, deep into the mountains, where he could have crossed at a number of passes — Great St Bernard, Little St Bernard, Mont Cenis or Clapier.

But more recently historians have speculated that the Carthaginian turned right before he got to the Isère and followed the Drôme River eastwards and then the smaller Durance River to the pass he eventually crossed: the high, desperate and snow-covered Col de la Traversette. This route fits very nicely with ancient sources. But it has been little studied in the field, mainly because until recently the Col de la Traversette was a smuggler's route that was quite dangerous to traverse, and there will be no agreement until archaeological evidence is found.

A POLYGLOT FORCE

Estimates vary regarding the size of Hannibal's army, but it was probably between 40,000 and 50,000, including 10,000 cavalry. This polyglot group (they spoke many languages) consisted of mercenaries, commanded by Carthaginian officers. Through extraordinary charisma, Hannibal managed to keep this diverse and polyglot force in line.

Famously, Hannibal also took forty war elephants with him. Elephants had already been used in combat for thousands of years and they were a potent force, the tanks or armoured cars of their time. They were especially effective against isolated communities that had never seen them before. Hannibal's elephants were African forest elephants. Now extinct, they were about half as high as the Asian elephant, although they were relatively speedy and more manoeuvrable.

Hannibal led his army out of New Carthage (the modern-day town of Cartagena on the east coast of Spain) in the spring of 218 BC, heading up the east coast to Gaul. He knew that he needed to make his journey in time to cross the Alps before winter set in. After crossing into Gaul and fighting off a warlike tribe near the Rhône River, Hannibal was alerted to the nearby presence of the Roman commander Scipio. This forced a change in Hannibal's plans. The more accessible passes in the Maritime Alps near the Mediterranean were now no longer an option as he felt sure the Roman fleet was dogging him. So he made a detour north, up the Rhône River, and then turned right and headed down a river valley through mountains that rose about 1500 metres high. It was now nearly the end of August, and he had little time left before the winter set in at high altitudes.

At this point, the strategy must have begun to seem reckless, even to the leader himself. Yet one of the reasons historians consider Hannibal such a brilliant leader is that he never once considered turning back, not even now when he knew the Romans were aware of his presence and he had lost the element of surprise.

As a young child Hannibal swore his allegiance to Carthage — and his eternal hatred of Rome.

★ ★ ★ ★ ★

INTO THE ALPS

After Hannibal made his stirring speech, his 40,000 or so men, along with elephants and horses and retainers, moved into the Alps. As the soldiers climbed, they wound their way through ever-narrower gorges and passes. Above them on cliff ledges were wild tribesmen, the Allobroges, whose shadowy presence was frightening. They soon launched an ambush that caught the Carthaginians in a narrow gorge. Hannibal bloodily repelled this onslaught.

After a week or so, Hannibal approached the tallest mountains in the French Alps, the last barrier between himself and the fertile valleys of Italy. These mountains were 4000 metres high, a truly awe-inspiring sight. The tribesmen who inhabited this region were even more threatening than the Allobroges. In his description of Hannibal's journey, the Roman historian Livy called them 'shaggy, unkempt men perched upon the crags above, more horrible to look at than words can tell'. In a bloody battle, the Carthaginians escaped their attempted ambush, aided in this by the elephants, which badly frightened the barbarians, sending them reeling out of the way when they charged.

★ ★ ★ ★ ★

A HIGH AND DESOLATE PASS

The hardest part of the journey was yet to come. The Carthaginians now had to cross one of the highest passes in the Alps. In attempting this, men by the hundreds, weak and exhausted, began to slip and fall — their cries echoed across the mountains. This was horrible music to the ears of those left climbing. According to one account, a snowstorm now hit the column, causing more men to stumble over the precipices.

Panic set in as the small amount of visibility began to dim. The roars of the elephants that thudded down the sides of the great peaks to their deaths were especially terrifying. The falling elephants were joined by many of the pack animals, who

This sixteenth century painting depicts the chaos of the Battle of Zama in 202 BC. It would prove to be Hannibal's last great battle with his old enemy, and it ended with the slaughter of the Carthaginians.

broke through the first soft layer of snow with their hooves, became stuck in the ice beneath and were finally pushed off the sides by soldiers impatient to get through. The soldiers themselves were burdened by supplies in heavy packs. One tilt off balance could send them, too, hurtling into the dark ravines that surrounded them.

FILTHY, EMACIATED AND TRAUMATISED, THEY MUST HAVE LOOKED WORSE THAN ANY OF THE 'BARBARIAN' PEOPLES WHO HAD TRIED TO STOP THEM. BUT THEY HAD MADE IT.

After three days, they reached the top of the pass and could look down upon the Po Valley of Italy. But the descent — down slippery, rocky slopes, where the back of the column trod on icy slush churned up by the front — cost even more lives than the climb. Finally, however, the army reached the lower slopes of the mountains, and entered a temperate zone — which must have seemed like Eden to them. Trees and grass grew in abundance and there was fresh game and fruit. Filthy, emaciated and traumatised, they must have looked worse than any of the 'barbarian' peoples who had tried to stop them. But they had made it.

★ ★ ★ ★ ★

TAKING THE BATTLE TO ROME

The cost of the journey had been high indeed. Estimates vary, but it appears that in the Alps Hannibal lost perhaps 20,000 men. Only three elephants — perhaps just one — survived.

Despite this, Hannibal had achieved his objective and was now in a position to attack the Romans. After resting his remaining 26,000 troops for nearly two weeks, Hannibal brought them to their feet and marched them south through Italy.

Hannibal was to spend the next fourteen years campaigning in Italy, where he won numerous victories. This included his bloody and historic success at Cannae in 216 BC, where his force massacred 50,000 Roman soldiers in one day. But he was never able to get the city-states of the Italian Peninsula to side with him, and Rome finally defeated Hannibal in 202 BC at the Battle of Zama, in North Africa.

Soon thereafter, the Carthaginian commander went into exile. Rather than be captured by the Romans, he committed suicide on an obscure island. Despite this, no one could say that Hannibal had ever really been defeated.

THE ASSASSINATION OF JULIUS CAESAR

[44 BC]

★ ★ ★ ★ ★ ★ ★ ★ ★ ★ ★ ★ ★ ★

The conspirators who killed in the name of democracy, and ended up destroying the Roman Republic

At dinner, Julius Caesar suddenly asked his companions what manner of death they might hope for, and answered his own question by saying he wanted a quick, unexpected end. After he went to bed, the windows and shutters of his house were blown open, as if by a fierce wind, except that the night was calm. In his sleep, Caesar dreamed he was flying above the clouds, lighter than air, and he awoke just as he was reaching out to touch the hand of Jupiter.

That morning was the Ides, or middle, of March. As Caesar rubbed the sleep out of his eyes, his wife, Calpurnia, told him that she had dreamed of his lifeless body lying bloody in her lap. She begged him not to go to meet with the Roman Senate, as he had planned to do. Her pleas gave him pause; Calpurnia was not prone to hysteria. Moreover, Caesar recalled the prophecy of soothsayer, Spurinna, that danger would befall him no later than the Ides of March.

Armed with daggers, Caesar's assassins surround him, slashing and stabbing in a frenzy.

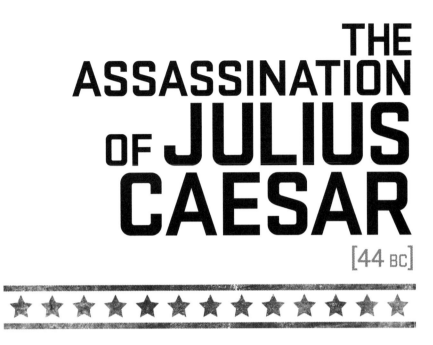

When Caesar's close aide Mark Antony arrived at his house, Caesar instructed him to postpone the visit. But then another friend arrived and convinced Caesar it would not be appropriate to cancel a meeting with the Senate. The friend's name was Decimus Brutus. He was a distant cousin of another Brutus who awaited Caesar on the Senate floor — and he had murder in his heart.

Caesar listened to this man and left his home for the last time.

★ ★ ★ ★ ★

A CAUTIONARY TALE?

The most significant figure in the thousand-year history of Ancient Rome, Gaius Julius Caesar was born in 100 BC in the month of Quintilis, a month that was later named after him: July. Caesar was altogether extraordinary. He was a brilliant military leader — brave, imaginative, beloved of his men — who advanced the fortunes of Rome immeasurably by conquering Gaul. He was also a fine writer, whose tales of his conquests, while sometimes self-serving, are always gripping. And he was a superb administrator who, despite being from a noble family himself, sought ways to spread the wealth of Rome around.

The story of Caesar's assassination continues to fascinate us as a study of political power and the complex ethical issues surrounding it. The achievements of Caesar, and his popularity at the time of his death, make his killing, on the face of it, puzzling. Yet the assassins claimed to be acting for the good of Rome. Can their act be justified? Is it acceptable to murder an individual or individuals for the benefit of the majority — is it justifiable, in other words, to kill in the name of democracy?

★ ★ ★ ★ ★

CONQUEROR OF ADVERSITY

As Caesar was carried by litter along the bustling streets of Rome, a man raced up to him holding a note and thrust it into his hands, begging him to read it. Caesar took the note and pocketed it, waving the man off. The note revealed a plot against Caesar, but Caesar had tucked the note away without reading it. Whether he felt any unease at this point, following the earlier warnings and dreams, we do not know.

SENSING THAT IT WOULD BE WISE TO SPEND SOME TIME AWAY FROM ITALY, HE JOINED THE ARMY. THUS BEGAN A DISTINGUISHED MILITARY CAREER THAT WOULD CATAPULT HIM TO POWER.

Caesar was a member of one of Rome's original aristocratic families, the Julii. Once ruled by kings, Rome now was ruled by an oligarchy, a group of noble families, the *nobilitas*. Though not part of this ruling aristocracy, the Julii were well connected — fortunately for Caesar. When he was only sixteen, he ran afoul of the tyrant Sulla. He joined a group that challenged aristocratic rule, favouring a more democratic approach — an early instance of Caesar's political leanings where he would identify with the interests of ordinary people. Sulla ordered Caesar's arrest, but Caesar escaped. Sensing that it would be wise to spend some time away from Italy, he joined the army. Thus began a distinguished military career that would catapult him to power.

When Sulla died in 78 BC, Caesar returned to Italy and built up a reputation as a politician. By 59 BC, he had gained the prestigious position of co-consul with Marcus Calpurnius Bibulus. However, true power lay with what modern historians

call the First Triumvirate, an informal alliance of three formed by Caesar with his allies Crassus and Pompey.

The members of the Senate and the most powerful aristocratic families were at this time broadly divided into two opposing camps. The *optimates* distrusted the populace and wanted to hold power close to the ruling oligarchies or noble families. The *populares*, the reformers, sought (or pretended to seek) to improve the lot of the common people. Caesar was a *popularis*, and as part of the First Triumvirate had tried to pass a law that redistributed land to the poor. This endeared him greatly to the underprivileged of Rome, the *proletarii*, or plebs. Was Caesar trying to create a power base for himself as a future dictator, as his enemies (and many historians) claimed? Or was he was a genuine populist reformer?

Caesar's heroic campaigns in Gaul (from 58 to 50 BC) won him, and Rome, great riches. They also served to create a strong power base among his loyal legions. He gave away large allotments of land (to 80,000 plebs in Rome and to thousands of army veterans) and set up public works projects such as draining marshes to provide work for the unemployed. On occasion, he even doled out cash to soldiers and citizens straight from the treasury.

There is now a very strong point of view that those who decided Caesar must be stopped and plotted his fall were in fact rich nobility out to stop what they feared would be a wholesale power shift from the haves to the have-nots. (Traditionally, historians have seen the plot that arose against Caesar as an attempt by patriotic, even democratic, Romans to stop a despot.)

This imposing statue of Caesar, 'the most significant figure in the thousand-year history of Ancient Rome', stands outside the Austrian Parliament in Vienna.

★ ★ ★ ★ ★

THE LIBERATORS

As Caesar travelled to the Senate on 15 March 44 BC, the men who would kill him waited nervously. The plot had begun with Gaius Cassius Longinus, who harboured an enormous grudge against Caesar. He saw him as a tyrant, but he may also have feared Caesar's rising popularity would weaken the powerful aristocracy, of which Cassius was a prominent member.

Cassius's most important ally was his brother-in-law, a young nobleman named Marcus Brutus, who happened to be the son of Caesar's longtime lover, Servilia. (He may have held grudges against Caesar that were personal rather than political.) The conspiracy then grew to include sixty mainly aristocratic Romans. One was Decimus Brutus, the distant cousin of Marcus, who was in fact a close friend of Caesar's. These men called themselves 'the Liberators', and, over a period of months leading up to March of 44 BC, met secretly. While, as senators, they denounced Caesar's supposed tyranny, they had a great deal to lose by Caesar's land distributions and his reforms. They feared that the great, unwashed rabble now following Caesar so slavishly might ultimately gain power and turn on them.

The conspirators decided to take drastic action on 15 March — the Ides of March — when Caesar would address the Senate.

★ ★ ★ ★ ★

'THE IDES OF MARCH HAVE COME!'

Accompanied by his friend Decimus Brutus, Caesar arrived in front of the Senate House mid-morning. He went up the steps of the Senate and onto the floor — without bodyguards, as usual, since he considered having them to be a sign of fear. The Senate stood in respect. Caesar sat down in his chair but almost immediately was surrounded by the conspirators, who began to ask him questions, to distract him. Suddenly, Tillius Cimber yanked Caesar's robe off his shoulders, a signal that the attack should begin (and a potent symbol, for his purple robe was the symbol of Caesar's dictatorship).

Against a backdrop of menacing clouds, Caesar's body is displayed to the crowd on the Senate steps. Anger and fear were to sweep through the city.

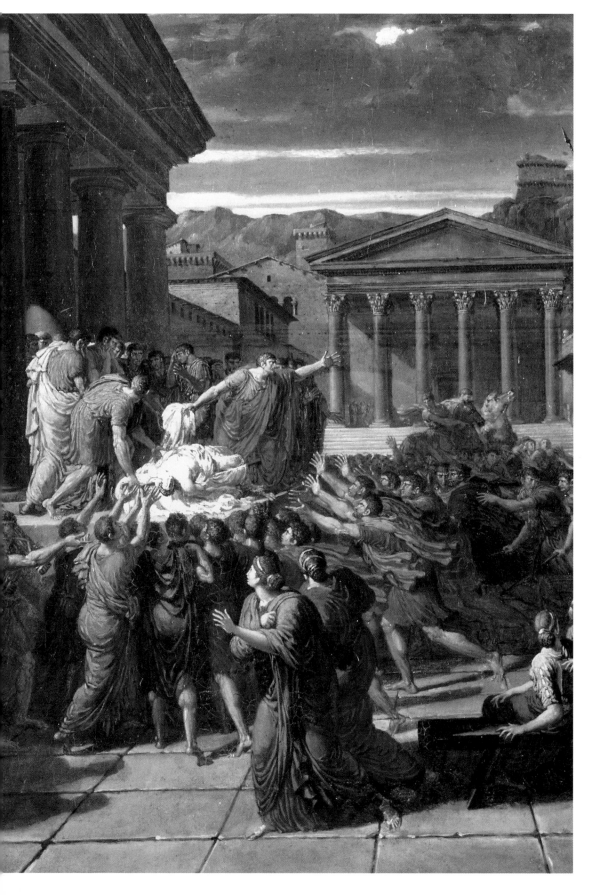

Trying to break through the circle of assassins that surrounded him, Caesar was stabbed in the face by Cassius. Then Decimus Brutus, who had lured him out that day, plunged a knife into his side. Whirling desperately, but trapped on all sides, Caesar fought as hard as he could. The assassins slashed and stabbed in a frenzy, so much so that they wounded several of their own members.

Marcus Brutus was one of the last to plunge his knife into Caesar. Shakespeare has the dying dictator cry, 'Et tu, Brutus?' but this is an invention. Suetonius claims that Caesar's last words, directed at Brutus, were, in Greek: 'And you too, my child!' Historian Plutarch merely says that Caesar wrapped his toga around his head and died at the foot of a statue of Pompey, with twenty-three stab wounds in his body.

★ ★ ★ ★ ★

IN WHOSE INTEREST?

Traditionally, Caesar has been portrayed as a man with a weakness for adulation. One step away from becoming a dictator, he was brought down by senators who feared for the integrity and survival of the Republic. In the last decade, however, some historians have questioned the motives of the assassins. They have convincingly claimed that Caesar in fact was one of a long line of democratic reformers killed by Roman oligarchs to protect their interests. The tribune Tiberius Gracchus was murdered in 133 BC by thugs hired by Roman aristocrats unhappy with Gracchus's land reforms. Yet another was Tiberius's brother, Gaius Gracchus, also a reformer, who was killed in 121 BC, along with 250 supporters, by death squads hired by the oligarchy.

UNINTENDED CONSEQUENCES

When they were done, the conspirators turned to the rest of the Senate, displaying their bloody knives and claiming that they had slain a dictator as a legitimate act of tyrannicide (tyrannicide being legal under Roman law). The terrified senators fled the Senate House. Anger and fear then swept through the city, paralysing Rome. By the next day, when Mark Antony gave his funeral oration for Caesar, the common people of the city had turned against the senators, even those who had not helped kill their idol.

Brutus and his co-conspirators were forced to flee the country. Thirteen years of civil war followed. In the end, the Roman Republic was no more. Imperial Rome, with Caesar's nephew Octavian as emperor, had begun, and would last for 500 years of absolute rule.

Were assassins acting out of self-interest or in a true belief that Rome faced a tyrant?

For six days after Caesar's violent death, a comet appeared in the skies above Rome. Some people believed it was Caesar's spirit, flying through the sky, as in his dream. And in coins minted after the assassination, the comet is always shown. That's a sign of the power of Caesar's name, then and thereafter, whether he was a tyrant or *popularis*, or a little of both.

THE **FALL** OF THE **ROMAN** **EMPIRE**

The beginning of Europe's long descent into darkness

The Roman Empire had a profound influence on the world today. Founded around 510 BC, the Empire had by the third century AD extended across millions of square kilometres, to the Rhine and Danube rivers in the north, North Africa in the south, Spain in the west and Constantinople and beyond in the east. Throughout this territory, the Romans paved roads (some still in use today) through wilderness, constructed towns and built aqueducts to water them. Roman government held sway and the Latin language grew in influence.

In 455 AD, Vandals spent two weeks sacking the city of Rome. This was a devastating blow to the might of the Roman Empire.

The city of Rome itself, with its public baths, sewer systems, glorious buildings and flourishing arts and poetry, was not only the centre of Western civilisation, but in a sense helped create it. Our Western systems of law, our cultures and our languages derive from ancient Rome. It is estimated that fifty per cent of the words in English, for example, are of Latin origin. Even our sense of empire. These days, it's considered a bad thing to have an empire, but Rome's thousand-year hold over the world probably did more good than harm.

Not surprisingly, the rulers of this magnificent empire attained godlike status. Some, such as Julius Caesar and Octavian, even claimed they were gods. So, given these great accomplishments, how did Rome end up in 476 AD being ruled by Romulus Augustus, a twelve-year-old boy?

★ ★ ★ ★ ★

BARBARIAN INVASIONS

The eighteenth century historian Edward Gibbon wrote a famous masterwork, *The History of the Decline and Fall of the Roman Empire*. He attributed Rome's 'fall' to two sources. Partly responsible were the 'barbarian' (from the Latin word for 'bearded') tribes who had long been bubbling and boiling around the edges of the northern Roman Empire. Sharing responsibility were the Romans themselves. Gibbon claimed they had become lazy and self-satisfied, depending on hired mercenaries to do their fighting (in some cases the same barbarians who would turn on them).

Many scholars today, however, view Gibbon's arguments about barbarian hordes as overly simplistic. Barbarians were, after all, mainly Germanic tribes on an empire-building mission of their own, who 'transformed' rather than 'destroyed' the empire. But this theory ignores the very real trauma felt by this thousand-year-old civilisation at the time. It also overlooks the impact of the decline of Western (read: Roman) learning that followed, when much classical knowledge was destroyed forever. As a result, Europe entered what has come to be known as the Dark Ages.

Romulus Augustus, the last emperor of Rome. After a short reign, he was deposed — as easily as a big kid pushes a little one out of the sandpit.

★ ★ ★ ★ ★

ROMVLVS · AVGVSTVS · I

...VSTVLVS, Orestis Patritij filius. Imperauit mens. IX. di
...XIV. sedente Simplicio. expulsus an. Chr. CDLXXVI

NEPOS DEPOSED

Romulus Augustus reigned from October of 475 to September of 476. Not much is known about him, except that he was thought good-looking. He was a kid caught in a big trap, really, one from which he was going to be lucky to escape alive, given the chaotic conditions in Rome at the time. Romulus had been named emperor by his father, a general named Flavius Orestes. The general was part German and part Roman. He had been named commander in-chief of the Roman army by the then-emperor, Julius Nepos.

This was a sign of the deep barbarian infiltration of Rome, and a mistake on Nepos's part. Orestes led a combined group of barbarian forces against the emperor, sending him into exile and putting his own son, Romulus, on the throne (probably so he could rule behind the scenes). But if he was expecting a bright new era in Roman history, or even just greater spoils, he was to be sorely mistaken.

★ ★ ★ ★ ★

A SLOW DECLINE

Rome had been sliding from power since the middle of the fourth century. The Huns, a nomadic people from Central Asia, had appeared on the Eurasian steppes and pushed other tribes westwards in front of them. One of these tribes was the Visigoths. They had settled on the banks of the Danube in about 376, living there with the grudging permission of Emperor Valens, head of the Eastern Roman Empire. (In 285, the Roman Empire had been divided into two halves, Eastern and Western, to make it easier to govern.)

Valens's corrupt officials treated the Visigoths in a high-handed way, as if they were inferiors, stealing money from them and not listening to their complaints. As a result, they revolted, and defeated and killed Valens in the historic battle of Adrianople in 378. Then they swept with a vengeance

THE FALL OF THE ROMAN EMPIRE

through the Eastern Empire. The next emperor, Theodosius I, finally made peace with the Visigoths in 382, but only after giving back the territory they had seized. Rome looked eastwards nervously.

Less than twenty years later, a charismatic young general named Alaric arose from one of the royal families of the Visigoths. Alaric was trained by the Emperor Theodosius and served as one of his top commanders, but after Theodosius died Alaric turned on the Romans. He first invaded Italy in 400, but was defeated. It is possible he invaded because the Romans had captured his wife and family and were holding them hostage. Alaric soon turned with purposeful vengeance and marched on Rome.

HE FIRST INVADED ITALY IN 400, BUT WAS DEFEATED. IT IS POSSIBLE HE INVADED BECAUSE THE ROMANS HAD CAPTURED HIS WIFE AND FAMILY AND WERE HOLDING THEM HOSTAGE. ALARIC SOON TURNED WITH PURPOSEFUL VENGEANCE AND MARCHED ON ROME.

In August 410, panic gripped the citizens of Rome as Alaric settled in for a siege. The Emperor Honorius fled just as Rome began to starve. Thousands of slaves left their masters and slipped out through the city's gates, seeking better employment with the Visigoths. Honorius refused to bargain with Alaric; meanwhile, the people of Rome, suffering from a plague, began to die by the scores. According to some sources, cannibalism was practised. Finally, someone — legend has it that it was a rich Roman noblewoman who could no longer

A thousand years after the fall of Rome, artists vividly portrayed the devastation of a great civilisation.

stand the plight of her city — opened the Salaria Gate, and, for the first time in 700 years, Rome was in the hands of a foreign invader.

As far as sackings went, Alaric's was relatively mild. Many Roman citizens were enslaved, but because of this there was a glut of slaves on the market and they could be bought back from the barbarians very cheaply.

IT IS A SIGN OF HOW INSIGNIFICANT A THREAT ROMULUS WAS THAT ODOACER DID NOT BOTHER TO HAVE HIM KILLED – HE SIMPLY PENSIONED HIM OFF TO CAMPANIA IN SOUTHERN ITALY.

What the Visigoths were mainly interested in was food. After obtaining what little they could from the starving Romans, they set off south to sack more fertile parts of the country. But Alaric died of an illness shortly thereafter, and the threat was temporarily dispelled.

★ ★ ★ ★ ★

THE EMPIRE DISINTEGRATES

Soon, however, it had to deal with Attila and his Huns, who had moved out of Asia pillaging and conquering. While they did not build great cities like the Romans, the Huns — particularly the charismatic Attila, who saw himself as a world leader — were intent on absorbing conquered peoples. After first invading the Balkans and Gaul, they headed for Italy. In 452, Attila cut a great swathe of destruction through the northern part of the country before heading for Rome. It is said that Pope

Leo I then met with Attila and persuaded him not to attack the city, although it is more likely that Attila turned back because famine and disease were by then tearing his army apart. In any event, Rome was spared.

Attila died the next year, and the power of the Huns waned, but in 453 the Vandals dealt Rome a devastating blow. The Vandals were a tribe from eastern Germany whose very name is now synonymous with wanton destruction. They took a roundabout route to Rome — through Spain, hopping across the Mediterranean, devastating North Africa and then sailing to Italy. They spent two full weeks sacking Rome, and did not refrain from murder and plunder, before returning to North Africa.

Over the next twenty years, the Imperial City and the Roman Empire disintegrated. The Italian Peninsula was devastated by barbarian onslaughts and civil war. The struggling Roman government was unable to levy enough taxes to keep a standing army in the field. Increasingly, it depended on barbarian mercenaries. The Roman government was weak and obviously up for grabs. It was at this point, 475, that Flavius Orestes was appointed — to protect the Roman emperor. As soon as he could, he betrayed him.

★ ★ ★ ★ ★

ROMULUS IN EXILE

After Flavius Orestes appointed Romulus emperor, he, too, fell prey to the tumultuous politics of the time. He had double-crossed the barbarians who had fought for him, refusing to give them land to settle on. The barbarians joined forces and rose against him, led by the Visigoth Odoacer (a name that has numerous spellings). Orestes was captured and quickly beheaded on 28 August 476. Then Odoacer marched on Ravenna, where Romulus Augustus held court. Odoacer deposed him immediately, as easily as a big kid pushes a little one out of a sandpit.

Odoacer then sent an arrogant note to Emperor Zeno of Constantinople, then head of the Eastern Empire. There would be no need to appoint a new Western emperor: he, Odoacer, would now rule. It is a sign of how insignificant a threat Romulus was that Odoacer did not bother to have him killed — he simply pensioned him off to Campania in southern Italy.

The fall of the Roman Empire was so quiet, one commentator has written, as to be 'noiseless'. But this was because by the time Odoacer pushed Romulus out, the power of Rome was already gone forever, lost in war and strife. The Eastern Empire was more fortunate, and survived until the fifteenth century. But the Western Empire was gone. For a time, Roman bureaucracy kept the streets paved, the water flowing through the aqueducts and the books safe in their grand libraries. However, these things were not of value to the new owners of the empire, and gradually fell into disuse and disrepair.

WHAT HAPPENED TO ROMULUS AUGUSTUS?

There is much speculation, but not a lot of real evidence, as to what happened to the young emperor after Odoacer deposed him. It is known that he went to live with relatives in Campania, in southern Italy, with a pension of 6000 gold *solidi* a year. He may have become a scholar or a monk — there is brief mention of a 'lovely letter by the holy brother Romulus' in correspondence, dated 507, between a North African bishop and an Italian diplomat. And around the same time, a secretary to Theodoric the Great wrote a letter to a Romulus about certain issues to do with a pension. But after this, all is silent.

Some aristocratic Roman families cooperated with the Germanic tribes and thrived, but many of the inhabitants of Rome and other major Italian cities were enslaved. Others were left alone to work for their new masters. But because the barbarians had redistributed the land among themselves, these former Roman citizens were left in a condition approaching serfdom.

Times changed. Coins were not minted. The famous Roman pottery, which had spread across the empire, was no longer made. Local economies declined severely, as did the population of Europe. The great civilisation of classical antiquity now entered a steady decline. The Dark Ages, which would last until about 1000, had begun.

Christopher Columbus's ships The Pinta, *the* Niña *and the*
Santa María *sail majestically towards the West Indies in 1492.*

THE MIDDLE AGES AND RENAISSANCE

[1000–1500]

MVSEVM
BRITAN
NICVM

Ego Willms cognoie Bastard Rex Anglie do z
qcedo tibi Nepoti meo Alano Brytanme Cõmti
z htredib; tuis nmpim omes villas z tras que
muv fueruit Comitis Edlbyni in Eboracsh;
z Isuetudib; ita libet honorifice sicut ide
Edlbin ica tenuit Ode in obsione eran
Cuntate Ebor

THE BATTLE OF HASTINGS

[1066]

★ ★ ★ ★ ★ ★ ★ ★ ★ ★ ★ ★ ★

The Norman triumph that changed the face of medieval England

The Earl of Brittany, kneeling at the feet of the newly crowned William the Conqueror, was one of many noblemen rewarded for their loyalty.

In the early light of the October morning, the Normans gazed up the crest of a hill at an impenetrable wall of Saxon shields. Behind the shields, were the English aristocrats, loyal to their Anglo-Saxon King Harold, covered with chain mail. They wore strong helmets, and carried swords and long, double-edged Danish axes. They had planted their heavy semicircular shields on the ground, interlocking them so that there was not a centimetre of space between them. Behind this barrier were the English peasants who, under the feudal system, were obliged to fight for their king. At the centre of the line, astride his horse and protected by his bodyguards, was King Harold Godwinson. It was his intention to hold firm and triumph, or die.

Lined up against the Saxons, at the foot of the hill, were the forces of the invader, William the Bastard of Normandy, soon to be known as William the Conqueror. William's forces were equal in number to the Saxons, but far more mobile and professional, for they included cavalry and archers, and experienced Italian mercenaries. It was William's intention to shatter the English shield wall, kill Harold and take his crown.

The battle began with a song. According to a legend, William's minstrel and knight, Ivo Taillefer, begged the honour of charging the English first. Speeding his horse towards the Saxons, Taillefer taunted them singing and tossing his sword in the air. When an enraged Saxon soldier charged out to challenge him, Taillefer decapitated him and took his head as a trophy — and as proof that God was on his side.

The Saxons believed differently, of course. As the Normans rushed up the hill, they shouldered close behind their shield wall and cried, 'Ut! Ut!' Meaning 'Out! Out!'.

★ ★ ★ ★ ★

THE MEN FROM THE NORTH

At this moment, around nine o'clock on the morning of 14 October 1066, the future of England hung in the balance. The Anglo-Saxons had controlled the country since the fifth century. Now, they were faced with a mass invasion of their lands by the Normans from northern France — who intended to stay.

WHEN AN ENRAGED SAXON SOLDIER CHARGED OUT TO CHALLENGE HIM, TAILLEFER DECAPITATED HIM AND TOOK HIS HEAD AS A TROPHY – AND AS PROOF THAT GOD WAS ON HIS SIDE.

The Normans had recently emerged as a formidable power in the region. They were descended from Vikings whose correct name, *Normanni*, means 'the men from the north'. Under the feudal system, tenant farmers and knights were obliged to fight for the landholders, providing manpower and supplies for the

Norman campaigns. However, this led to an unceasing quest for more land. By the mid-eleventh century, England, just a short distance across the English Channel, had become a tempting target. All the more so because the Duke of Normandy saw himself as the country's rightful ruler.

★ ★ ★ ★ ★

A PROMISE AND AN OATH

Strong links already existed between England and Normandy. The previous ruler, King Edward the Confessor, had spent twenty-five years in exile in Normandy. On his return to England, he had taken with him a group of Norman advisers. This upset the Anglo-Saxon aristocracy, who gave their support to Godwin of Wessex, a powerful English lord. Aided by William, Edward expelled Godwin from the country. On Godwin's death, his son, Harold Godwinson returned to England. Harold became increasingly influential, so much so that King Edward — not the most strong-willed of rulers — made him a chief adviser.

In 1064, Harold was shipwrecked off the French coast and captured by the Duke of Normandy. William claimed that Edward had promised England to *him* in 1051 in return for his aid in expelling Godwin. He forced Harold to swear an oath to support his 'claim' to the throne once Edward died. Edward, however, denied making any promises to William. So, following Edward's death on 5 January 1066, there being no other heir to the throne, and with the full support of the kingdom's most powerful nobles, Harold was crowned king at Westminster Abbey.

This infuriated William. And William was not a person to trifle with. Sincerely believing that God was on his side, he resolved to amass a great seaborne army, take England by force and depose Harold.

★ ★ ★ ★ ★

This Bayeux Tapestry detail shows Harold's brothers, Gyrth and Leofwine,
felled by Norman cavalry and archers. Their shields lie useless beside them.

HAROLD BESIEGED

William's invasion fleet was an incredible one for the time — 600
ships, which were to hold 7000 men in all, including knights,
archers and infantry. For months, the coast of Normandy rang

with these shipbuilding efforts. The fleet was finished in early September, and when favourable winds arose on the 27th, William and his men set sail for England.

King Harold already had his hands full, because he was fighting off not one invasion force, but two. For there was another claimant to the throne, King Harald III Sigurdsson of Norway. Harald invaded England in September, landing in the north-east and defeating the armies of two northern earls before making camp near York. Harold reacted swiftly, marched north with his army and, on 25 September, emerged the victor. This was a major victory for England, and also marked the last time a Scandinavian army would attempt to invade the country.

William landed on the south-east coast of England three days later. Needing as quick a victory as possible, since he was operating on foreign territory, far from his base of supply, he and his forces began pillaging the land, hoping to draw Harold into battle. It worked: Harold raced down from York, stopped in London to gather more forces and then headed with all speed to the little village of Hastings, in East Sussex. There he arrayed his forces across the Hastings–London road, on Senlac Hill, a site now known as Battle Hill.

Harold had 7000 men set up across the crest of the hill, their flanks anchored on either side by woods, with the massive forest of Anderida at his back. But Harold's forces were not as strong as they seemed, as they had been weakened both by losses at the Battle of Stamford Bridge and by the reluctance of local peasants to fight another pitched battle.

★ ★ ★ ★ ★

'I'M ALIVE!'

After Ivo Taillefer made his fabled charge, William gave a command and a shower of arrows fell upon the English. Norman archery tactics depended on shooting back arrows already fired by opponents, and since the Saxons were without archers, the Normans were soon forced to stop firing in order to conserve their ammunition.

William then had his infantry charge straight up the hill at the densely packed English army. But these foot soldiers were unable to break through the shield wall and fell back, with many dead and wounded. A rumour then rippled through the panicky Norman ranks that William was dead and he was forced to doff his helmet and ride in front of his lines, yelling, 'I'm alive! I'm alive!' But he was faced with a problem. The longer the battle took, the more likely it would be that reinforcements would come to Harold's aide. As the day wore on, repeated attacks on the shield wall produced nothing but dead Normans.

★ ★ ★ ★ ★

AN ARROW IN THE EYE?

By late afternoon, the battle had come down to a bitter, brutal clash of two armies. The shield wall had fallen back on itself and tightened up as losses increased. But still the English and King Harold held on. William knew that if night fell and he had still not found a way through the shield wall, he would be forced to retreat.

THE BAYEUX TAPESTRY

A depiction of the events surrounding the Norman Conquest of England, the Bayeux Tapestry (see detail on pages 50–51) is one of the most extraordinary artifacts we have from this era. Preserved now in Bayeux, France, it is extremely long and narrow — 70 metres by 0.5 metre wide. It is not actually a woven tapestry, but a piece of cloth embroidered with panels, each showing a particular event. It was probably commissioned in the 1070s by Bishop Odo, William the Conqueror's half-brother, as a way of commemorating William's victory — and as a handy piece of propaganda, since the Norman point of view is the only one shown. As a source of information on medieval society and soldiery at the time, it has been invaluable to modern scholars.

In this nineteenth century painting, Harold's body is brought before William the Conqueror. Harold's death marked the end of Anglo-Saxon rule in Britain.

Before preparing for one last assault, he ordered his archers to shoot another volley, this one high over the Saxon lines, where it fell, creating havoc among the closely packed forces. As the Normans advanced, King Harold, who was rallying his troops, looked up into the sky and was pierced by an arrow that hit him directly in the eye. Some stories have it that he pulled it out and continued fighting, half-blind, blood pouring down his face, flanked by his bodyguards, until he was cut down by a Norman knight. But there are numerous versions of Harold's end, some of which have his body hacked to pieces. The Bayeux Tapestry shows a figure being struck through the eye with an arrow.

However it happened, Harold died on the field, and the Saxons, having no king left to fight for, fled. William was triumphant: England was his. Courage is an essential attribute for a king and William certainly had that — three horses were killed under him that day. But so is luck. And William's luck may well have included an arrow that found its way to the eye of the king of England.

★ ★ ★ ★ ★

A FUSION OF CULTURES

Since there was no one left in England who was strong enough to oppose William, he had himself crowned king on Christmas Day, 1066. With the Norman Conquest complete, England changed forever. Land was given to the Norman lords who had participated in the conquest, a traumatic process for the Saxon owners. However, the Normans left intact the Anglo-Saxon legal system — sheriffs, courts, taxes and names of counties.

In the longer term, the Norman invasion changed the English language — infusing it with French and Latin — and ensured that Catholicism would be the state religion (until the sixteenth century). The Saxons had trouble adapting to the rule of the man they considered a tyrant. Yet was William such a tyrant? Although he met the fierce resistance of the north of England after Hastings with blood and fire, he also knew when to be merciful, and he understood how to administer and apply laws.

William the Conquerer died in 1087, still holding the lands he had conquered. No one really knows what would have happened had William failed to conquer England, but the melding together of these two strong peoples created one of the most extraordinary cultures in the Western world.

et austres sains lieux la cruon. miaultes. Et comment Jlz
Et les ypiens phabitans ꝯ demou les tenoient en trop opprobrieuse
tans . ꝯ que les austres par eulx captiuite ꝯ seruaige . ou tresgrant
tyranniquement ꝯ Inhumaine deshonneur ꝯ opprobre de tous
ment tues . Jl auoient reserue les ypiens . Concluant ꝯ mon
en Jnselicieuse vie a fin que sur strant par diuerses raisons tres
eulx en lopprobre du saint nom euidentes que le saint peuple
ypien peussent continuer plus ypien ne debuoit plus souffrir
longuement leurs Jnsaciables nenditer que les sains lieux et

THE
CRUSADES

★ ★ ★ ★ ★ ★ ★ ★ ★ ★ ★ ★ ★ ★

The centuries-long battle for the Holy Land that left a legacy of suspicion and misunderstanding

On a cold November day in 1095, Pope Urban II gave a powerful speech in France. It had a momentous impact on both the history of Europe and the Middle East. The pope had received an urgent plea for help from Emperor Alexius. The Muslim Turks were threatening Constantinople, the eastern stronghold of Christianity in Asia Minor.

Of even greater concern to the pope was their threat to the Holy City of Jerusalem.

'The Arabs have occupied more and more of the lands of those Christians,' he addressed his audience. 'They have killed and captured many, and have destroyed the churches and devastated the empire ... I, or rather the Lord, beseech you as Christ's heralds ... to carry aid promptly to those Christians and to destroy that vile race from the lands of our friends.'

Urban whipped the crowd into a frenzy, promising them that 'all who die by the way, whether by land or by sea, or in battle against the pagans, shall have immediate remission of sins'. His listeners shouted over and over again, *Deus lo volt!* — 'God wills it!' And so the Holy Wars began.

The impact of Pope Urban II's powerful address to cardinals, knights and noblemen was no doubt heightened by the splendour of Clermont's cathedral.

★ ★ ★ ★ ★

A MIXED LEGACY

The popular view of the Crusades in the West was shaped first by the romantic literature that sprang up during the Crusades, and later by Hollywood. Early on, Crusaders were portrayed as soldiers of God on a divine mission to reclaim the Holy Land. However, in literature and in films today, these European knights are more likely to be presented as bloodthirsty thugs out only for gold and land. Nevertheless, the extraordinary importance of the Crusades in history remains. Scholar Thomas F. Madden has written that 'whether we admire the Crusaders or not, it is a fact that the world we know today would not exist without their efforts'.

In the century before the Crusades, Christian Western Europe was recovering from the ravages of the Dark Ages and fighting off attacks from various invaders — including Muslim peoples from North Africa (some of whom were fighting their way up the Iberian Peninsula). Meanwhile the popes were seeking a way to turn Europe's nobles away from their internal squabbles — and confront the threat of Islam in the Holy Land.

★ ★ ★ ★ ★

AN ELECTRIFYING EFFECT

Pope Urban II repeated his speech several times throughout 1095 and 1096. He sent forth his clergy to spread the word all over Europe: all who wanted to fight the Muslims were to swear a pilgrim's oath and make their way to Constantinople by 15 August 1096. From there they would set out for the Holy Land. In return, they would be granted indulgences for the remission (or forgiveness) of their sins.

Over 100,000 people joined the initial wave of the First Crusade, known as the 'Peasants' Crusade'. A huge number of peasants and land-poor knights streamed east towards Constantinople. They saw their pilgrim's oath as a sure road out of their impoverished lives. A charismatic monk known as

Peter the Hermit was one of their leaders. Peter, preaching throughout northern France, told mass gatherings of peasants to meet in Cologne, Germany, in April, well ahead of Urban's proposed rendezvous. Leaving from there in two different groups, this ragtag Crusade headed for Byzantium.

★ ★ ★ ★ ★

RIVAL RELIGIONS

Jerusalem has long been a city holy to both Christians and Muslims. The Muslims knew it as al-Quds ('the Holy Place'). When they captured it in 638 AD, they built one of the world's most beautiful places of worship there: the Dome of the Rock.

OVER 100,000 PEOPLE JOINED THE THE FIRST CRUSADE ... PEASANTS AND LAND-POOR KNIGHTS STREAMED EAST TOWARDS CONSTANTINOPLE.

However, the idea that European Christians simply set out at the end of the eleventh century to retake Jerusalem for no reason other than fervent anti-Islamic sentiment doesn't portray the entire picture. For, at the time, Islam did pose a very real threat to Christianity.

The older of the two religions, Christianity had arisen in the first century AD and spread to all parts of the Roman Empire (which then included Jerusalem and Palestine, out of which the Romans had pushed the Jews). By the seventh century, when Islam began to flourish on the Arabian Peninsula, the religion of Jesus Christ was the predominant belief in Europe and the Mediterranean basin.

But not for long. Muslim forces took over Palestine, Syria and Egypt, crossed to Spain, and defeated Christian forces (the Muslims knew the European Christians as 'Franks') on the Iberian Peninsula. By the mid-eighth century, they had launched raids into France.

Conflict between the two groups continued for the next 200 years. When the Turks threatened the Byzantine Empire, the Emperor Alexius I Comnenus made a plea for help to Western Europe. It was this plea that prompted Urban's speech.

Crusaders do battle with Saracens. Saladin was the most ferocious leader of his age, a Saracen warrior-king who drove the Christians from Jerusalem.

DESTRUCTION OF THE PEASANTS' ARMY

The undisciplined army of pilgrims made its way across the Rhineland in the spring of 1096. One group participated in horrific slaughters of Jews — whom they considered to be enemies of Christ — in the German towns of Metz (now a part of France), Worms and Mainz. The tattered army took on a force of veteran Turks a short distance from Constantinople, and was quickly demolished.

A much more formidable group of soldiers led by great European nobles was to follow. Motivated by religious ideals, these men put aside their differences, raised a powerful army of knights, and made the long, extremely arduous journey to the Holy Land. There they wrested Jerusalem from the Muslims in 1099. When the Crusaders entered the city, they massacred Muslims and Jews alike.

THE SECOND CRUSADE

The First Crusade had been successful beyond anyone's dreams. It saw the Holy Land liberated in near record time, opening Jerusalem to Christian pilgrims and founding a new Christian realm in Palestine. Palestine consisted of a narrow finger of land between the Mediterranean Sea and the Jordan River. This sliver of Christianity was surrounded by enemies, notably the Seljuk Turks in Syria in the north and Fatimid Egypt in the south.

On Christmas Day, 1144, a Seljuk leader attacked the northernmost of the Crusader States in Palestine, and murdered all of its European Christian inhabitants. This prompted the ill-fated Second Crusade, which was nearly a complete disaster. One of the lowest points was a foolish attack on Damascus, a Muslim-controlled city that had, up to that point, been a supporter of Christian Jerusalem. The Christian forces retreated in disarray.

Heartened by this victory, Islamic forces began to attack Crusader outposts. And so the pattern for years of warfare was set, with Crusader castles being besieged by 'Saracens', and other Crusaders riding to the rescue. ('Saracens', which came from a Greek term meaning 'easterners', was the name given to the Muslims by the Franks.) Slowly, the Saracens whittled away the Christian holdings in the Holy Land.

In 1174, a new leader gained power, Salah al-Din Yusuf Ibn Ayyub. He was known to history as Saladin, the most ferocious Islamic leader of his age (or of almost any other). Saladin portrayed himself as the unifier of Muslims and set out to drive the Christians from the Holy Land.

He defeated two armies sent from Jerusalem, near Galilee, finally entering Jerusalem in triumph in 1187. After this, only a few Christian cities held out, notably the port city of Tyre. Saladin had, for the time being, stamped out the foreign presence in his land.

★ ★ ★ ★ ★

THE THIRD CRUSADE

The Third Crusade is probably the best known in the popular imagination of both West and East. It was dominated by two famous warrior-kings, Saladin and King Richard I, the Lionheart, of England. With the Crusader States in Palestine teetering on the edge of extinction, Richard joined forces with Emperor Frederick Barbarossa of Germany and King Philip II of France.

From the beginning, the Third Crusade was marred by ill fortune. Frederick fell off his horse and drowned while crossing the Saleph River in Anatolia. Richard and Philip, once the closest of friends, began arguing as they sailed to the Holy Land. Once there, they managed to retake the city of Acre from Saladin — but Philip, ill and unhappy, then left the Crusade.

Richard was to become himself the leader history and folklore has painted him: bold, intelligent and extremely brave.

Richard I was known for his courage on the battlefield. This English hero, whose home was in Aquitaine, France, actually spoke very little English.

He swept along the coast of Palestine, leading his men to victory after victory. But whenever he struck inland to attack Jerusalem, he was unable to secure his supply lines against his marauding enemy. Ultimately, he was forced to make a truce with Saladin. Saladin would allow unarmed Christian pilgrims free access to the Holy City—but only on condition that Richard and his forces left the Holy Land.

★ ★ ★ ★ ★

THE CHILDREN'S CRUSADES

There were numerous 'popular crusades' during the years of crusading. These are crusades that arose spontaneously, not at the call of a pope, but simply as a fervent expression of faith. The most famous one is the so-called Children's Crusade of 1212, which was actually two separate crusades. The first began in Germany when a youth named Nicholas proclaimed that an angel had appeared to him and told him to gather a force and take back the Holy Sepulchre from the Saracens. Soon, 7000 youths followed him to Genoa. Once there, they expected the Mediterranean to part in front of them. When it did not, they returned home, disappointed.

The second was led by a shepherd boy named Stephen, who said he had a letter from Christ to the King of France. Stephen led 30,000 people to Paris to meet with the king, but when the letter was found to be a fake, the crusade dispersed.

No Children's Crusade reached the Holy Land. Scholars have even questioned whether such crusades really involved only children, since the word *pueri*, used by chroniclers to describe these groups, may also have meant a low-born person, no matter what his or her age.

THE LATER CRUSADES

There were four more Crusades in the thirteenth century, but none was ultimately successful. By 1291, the date conventionally given as the end of the Crusades, Islamic forces had succeeded in ousting all Christian forces from the former Crusader States. The Middle East was now completely controlled by Islamic rulers and would remain that way until the nineteenth century. However, the battle between Christianity and Islam went on elsewhere for hundreds of years.

It was Europe that benefited the most from the Crusades. Exposure to Islamic science, mathematics, art and military science invigorated European culture. The increased traffic between Europe and the Holy Land stimulated trade, and Europe came to better the Islamic world economically. In contrast, a resentful Islamic world retreated into isolation, the once sophisticated courts of the Muslim realms becoming cultural and economic backwaters.

Today, nearly 800 years after they officially ended, the Crusades are still a matter of speculation and controversy. Just after the terrorist attacks of September 11 2001, President George W. Bush referred in a speech to 'this crusade, this war on terrorism'. To many in the Islamic world, this evoked the spectre of Christian knights, invaders of Muslim lands who had set out to destroy a religion and a way of life. And so perhaps the most lasting effect of the Crusades was to have sown the seeds of an enduring suspicion between Islam and Christianity.

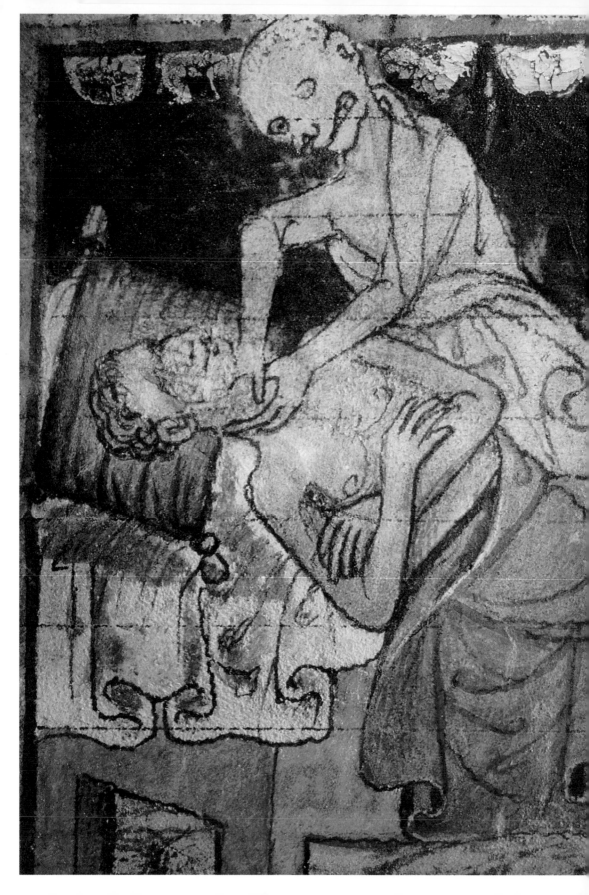

THE
BLACK DEATH

★ ★ ★ ★ ★ ★ ★ ★ ★ ★ ★ ★ ★ ★ ★

The devastating plague that still shadows us

This dramatic representation shows Death strangling its helpless and resigned victim. It was painted in 1376, barely three decades after the scourge had ended.

All over Europe, doctors refused to heal the sick, priests ran from the dying whose souls they were supposed to save and parents fled their children. People ate and drank in manic desperation and indulged in forbidden pleasures. In Italy, people lay with their faces over foul and bubbling sewers, hoping that the stench they inhaled would somehow ward off the dreaded disease. In England, people tore their clothes off and marched through the streets, whipping themselves with lashes.

In five years, beginning in 1347, one-third of Europe — twenty-five million people — died in the bubonic plague. Even this figure does not reflect the true horror of the situation, for many villages and towns lost eighty per cent of their populations. A world that had burst forth from the Dark Ages and was moving forwards into a new era suddenly found itself pockmarked with deserted farms, abandoned villages, collapsed churches and zombie-like survivors. Two centuries later, the name Black Death was coined for this pestilence ('black' referring not to the colour, but to something awful or evil). At the time it was sweeping across Europe it became known as the Big Death.

★ ★ ★ ★ ★

A DEVILISH DISEASE

Bubonic plague changed the course of world history and haunts humankind to this day. All subsequent epidemics — smallpox, cholera, influenza, AIDS — are a reminder of the terror of the Black Death, the spectre of a world strewn with dead bodies, defenceless against an invisible killer. Even with today's advanced medical treatment, with every new epidemic — be it AIDS or swine flu — we subconsciously fear the return of the Big Death.

BUBONIC PLAGUE WAS CAUSED BY DIRECT CONTACT WITH THE FLEAS AND RESULTED IN EGG-SHAPED LUMPS, OR BUBOES, AT THE SITE OF THE FLEA BITE, USUALLY IN THE ARMPIT OR GROIN AREA.

For those experiencing this extraordinary plague in the mid-fourteenth century, the effect was horrific. No wonder they whipped themselves, praying to God or trying to appease the devil. Though it wasn't known at the time, the devil in this case was a hardy rat flea known to scientists as *Xenopsylla cheopis*, a ravenous little creature that lived (sometimes by the hundreds) on black rats and other rodents. *X. cheopis* carried a virulent bacterium known as *Yersinia pestis*. When *X. cheopis* chomped down on human flesh (increasingly likely as rats began to die off, either from the plague or from hunger), *Y. pestis* entered the human body. The effects were deadly. Its victims died within five to seven days.

The illness caused by *Y. pestis* took two forms. Bubonic plague was caused by direct contact with the fleas and resulted in egg-shaped lumps, or buboes, at the site of the flea bite, usually in the armpit or groin area. Black-purple bruising followed, with a horribly foul stench arising from the victim. It killed six out of every ten people. But the main form of the medieval plague seems to have been the pneumonic variety. It infects the lungs and is then spread from person to person through the air, without the aid of *X. cheopis*. An Italian priest, writing in 1348, quite accurately depicted the course of pneumonic plague: '[The victims] began to spit blood and then they died — some immediately, some in two or three days … And it happened that whoever cared for the sick caught the disease from them or, infected by the corrupt air, became rapidly ill and died in the same way.'

A CREEPING PESTILENCE

By the beginning of the 1300s, populations in Europe had grown rapidly and urban centres were thriving and densely inhabited. At the same time, advances in shipbuilding and navigation sent traders far across the known world. But soon after the start of the fourteenth century, Europe was hit by devastating storms and frigid weather. Crops were destroyed and, in about 1315, a famine struck Northern Europe, which significantly weakened the survivors' immune systems.

Meanwhile, deep in Asia, bubonic plague was beginning its march. China's lengthy and bloody war against the Mongols destroyed vast tracts of countryside. No longer able to feed themselves in the forests, rats headed for populated areas. As the rats starved and died, *X. cheopis* sought new hosts. The humans they encountered, their immune systems weakened by starvation, other diseases and stress, were perfect targets. By the 1330s, the plague had laid China to waste. Historians estimate that China lost 35 million people out of a total population of about 125 million. Some scholars go further and say that one out of every two people in China died.

Near the end of the 1330s, *X. cheopis* began to travel. It went with traders as they followed well-worn routes westwards across the wide plains of Mongolia and Central Asia. By the spring of

1347, it had travelled to the outskirts of the town of Caffa on the north shore of the Black Sea. Caffa was a bustling trading centre where goods, people and ideas from East and West met. When traders from Genoa fell out with the local Mongol ruler, he laid siege to their town; but soon *X. cheopis* hit his troops and the soldiers succumbed by the thousands. So as to make his Genoese enemies share his pain, the Mongol leader ordered the stinking, plague-ridden bodies of his dead to be catapulted into Caffa, and the Christians inside began to die.

The decimated Mongol army finally gave up the siege and left. The panicked Genoese fled, boarding ships and heading across the Black Sea for Italy. They stopped at Constantinople and other ports, spreading the plague into each town, and then finally arrived in Italy in the autumn of 1347. As the ships from Caffa pulled into the port town of Messina, in Sicily, those onshore were horrified. There had been vague rumours of this horrible pestilence in the East, but now, here it was, right before their eyes. The Italian priest later wrote that the sailors in these dozen or so ships carried 'such a disease in their bodies that if anyone so much as spoke with one of them he was infected ... and could not avoid death'.

★ ★ ★ ★ ★

DEADLY TENTACLES REACH OUT

The Big Death resembled a many-tentacled monster holding the world in a dreadful embrace. One tentacle reached south and west from Constantinople to cause horrible suffering in Damascus, Jerusalem and Cairo. Another groped northwards from Messina, reaching central and northern Italy in early 1348. Not surprisingly, the plague tended to follow medieval trade routes.

The Italian writer Giovanni Boccaccio (1313–75) lived through the plague in the city of Florence. He brilliantly captured the experience in his famous *Decameron*, the story of ten well-born young people trapped by the pestilence in a

Flagellants believed that by whipping themselves they would atone for the sins of the world and escape a swift and horrible death.

villa. In the introduction to this work, Boccaccio describes the terror in the city, where people were afraid 'to speak or go near the sick' or even to touch their clothing. Some retreated from the world 'forming small communities … shutting themselves up in their houses ... avoiding all excess'. Others did exactly the opposite, thinking 'the sure cure for plague was to drink and be merry'. Neither approach did much good, though: the Black Death killed three-quarters of the population of Florence.

★ ★ ★ ★ ★

DECIMATED POPULATIONS

From Italy, the plague travelled north into Germany, and west to France and Spain. From France, the pestilence leaped across to southern England, landing there in the summer of 1348. It probably entered the country through the port of Bristol, which lost half its population, and then spread outwards, flourishing in the foul conditions of most medieval towns of the era, where sanitation was highly primitive. The disease arrived in London in November. Those who became infected lived scarcely two or three days, and soon London had lost one-third to one-half of its population. While the plague was a democratic killer — three Archbishops of Canterbury died, one after another — generally the poor died faster than the rich. This was no doubt because immune systems were undermined by poor nutrition. It was noted at the time: 'The one who was poorly nourished with unsubstantial food fell victim to the merest breath of the disease'.

Even harder hit were the villages of rural England, where a community of, say, 200 people might be wiped out. Historians estimate that the population of England and Wales in the early fourteenth century, before the plague struck, was six million people. It's possible that the plague killed fifty per cent of this population; numbers did not rise to the same level again until the mid-seventeenth century.

★ ★ ★ ★ ★

FINDING A SCAPEGOAT

Beginning mainly on the European mainland, in the spring of 1348, the plague brought about what has been called 'one of the most vicious outbreaks of anti-Semitic violence in European history'. Desperate for someone to blame, people claimed that the traditional outcasts, the Jews, had been putting poison into water wells. (Interestingly enough, fewer Jews may indeed have died of the Black Death, probably because they tended to shun outsiders, and kosher practices led to better personal hygiene and cleaner food.)

The hysteria reached a frenzied height with organised massacres against the two and a half million Jews who then lived in Europe. Kangaroo courts sprang up, sentencing Jews to death (burning at the stake was a favourite method) or exiling them and seizing their wealth and property.

In certain German cities, like Strasbourg (now in France), hundreds of Jews were burned to death after being stripped naked and having their clothes searched for hidden money — an omen perhaps of a greater holocaust that was to come centuries later.

A WORLD TRANSFORMED

The plague continued through England to Scotland, leaping to touch eastern Ireland, then crossing the North Sea to Scandinavia, before devastating Moscow in 1352 and heading further south. Finally, it died out (for the time being) near Kiev — exhausting itself on the endless and relatively empty Russian steppes.

The world was devastated, but the plague had brought a strange blessing. Europe had been overpopulated as the 1300s began, with people beginning to fight over resources. Now, there was a ghastly amount of room. The few remaining farm workers

were much in demand and could therefore insist on better wages and conditions. As a result, the standard of living of ordinary country dwellers improved.

One response to the Big Death was to live life to the fullest — men and women began to marry and start families earlier. Others became obsessed with death and dying. Morality plays became popular. They would be followed by a sermon, its message usually close to the inscription from a tomb of the period: 'Dust you are, unto dust you return, rotten corpse, morsel and meal to worms.'

The plague continued in numerous smaller yet still devastating recurrences for centuries thereafter, right up until the 1600s. Another wave swept through Asia late in the nineteenth century. Although this last plague pandemic was contained, *X. cheopis* still exists in wild rodents, and hundreds of plague cases are reported each year. These can be treated with antibiotics and further global outbreaks have been kept at bay, but the dreaded fear of the Big Death still remains.

The plague did not discriminate. Here, monks with the plague are blessed by a priest.

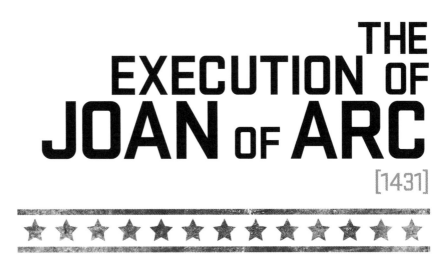

THE EXECUTION OF JOAN OF ARC

[1431]

★ ★ ★ ★ ★ ★ ★ ★ ★ ★ ★ ★ ★ ★ ★

How an illiterate peasant girl led her country to victory, and became a national, religious and feminist icon

Pushing and shoving to obtain the best vantage points, 10,000 spectators gathered in the main square of Rouen, in north-western France, on the morning of 30 May 1431. For weeks, they had watched the trial of the Maid at the hands of her merciless inquisitors and heard ever more outlandish stories of her past. At the centre of the square were four large platforms. On one sat the Maid's judges, on another her guards, on the third the Maid herself alongside her preacher, and on the last a wooden stake. This was planted in a moulded plaster base – to raise it high, so that it was visible to everyone in the crowd.

Before the Maid was brought to the stake, several ceremonies, sermons, speeches and prayers were performed. It all took so long that some of the eighty English soldiers guarding the Maid began to taunt her and the cleric who was praying with her: 'What, priest, will you make us dine here?' Finally, however, the Maid was chained to the post, with her arms high above her, and the crowd gasped as the wood was set ablaze.

This portrait of Joan of Arc shows her as both warrior and saint.

★ ★ ★ ★ ★

THE VARIOUS LEGACIES OF JOAN

Saint, heretic, illiterate shepherd girl, saviour of France, or psychologically disturbed — you can take your pick when it comes to Joan of Arc. She has been the subject of countless studies, and the leading character of novels, plays and operas, an inspirational symbol of courage for widely different groups. In 1920, the Catholic Church elevated the Maid to sainthood and held her up as an icon of both womanly purity and strength. And all this for an illiterate country girl who was perhaps nineteen when she died. Yet the essence of who Joan of Arc really was continues to elude us — just as it did her inquisitors.

★ ★ ★ ★ ★

CAPTURE OF THE 'SORCERER'

Inspired by her visions, Joan of Arc had fought successful battles against the British, who had long been rivals of France. When she fell into the hands of the English occupiers at Rouen in 1430, it was as if she had been taken by the devil, for these men meant to do her a great deal of harm.

The English wanted to put to death this 'sorcerer', as they called her, for she had been a great hindrance to their efforts to conquer France. In particular, she had been instrumental in making sure the French dauphin, or heir to the throne, became king. However, the English did not want to execute the Maid themselves and invite the disapproval of the many French people who sympathised with her. Therefore, they brought together a panel of judges and had them try her on religious grounds, for heresy (a crime punishable by death). For this, after all, was a woman who said God spoke to her on a daily basis.

★ ★ ★ ★ ★

VOICES IN BELLS

Joan of Arc (Jeanne d'Arc) was born, probably in January of 1412, to Jacques d'Arc and Isabelle Romée, at Domrémy on the Meuse River where the family owned a small amount of land. With her sister and brother, Joan grew up helping to farm and to tend flocks, although she proved to be hopeless when it came to chores. This was partly because of her piety, which made itself evident when she was very young. Whenever a bell sounded for Mass, she would drop whatever she was doing and head for the village church.

By the time Joan was thirteen or so, these innocent village bells signified something else: when the child heard them, she also heard voices from God. The voices (later accompanied by physical manifestations) were mainly those of three saints: St Michael, St Catherine and St Margaret. Eventually, these voices informed her that she needed to save France — a country that, at the time, was quite in need of a miracle or two.

Joan of Arc grew up towards the end of the Hundred Years' War, when the English fought for control of France. A vicious struggle for power was taking place, with one French faction siding with the English against the real heir to the French throne, the Dauphin Charles, son of Charles VI.

Into this desperate and chaotic situation stepped Joan, at the age of perhaps sixteen. Her saints had told her to drive the English out of France and ensure that the dauphin would be crowned king. Joan sought a meeting with the dauphin and he agreed to meet her. She had now begun to dress in men's clothes (including armour, shield and sword) in order to fit in with the rest of the army. She was supremely confident that the English siege of the key city of Orléans, with her help, could be turned into a French victory.

Indeed, Joan not only lifted the siege at Orléans (despite being wounded by a crossbow bolt in the neck), she also helped capture several other towns in the English-occupied zone. She finally escorted the dauphin to be crowned King Charles VII at Reims. She had achieved her first major military victory.

How did this peasant girl acquire enough military leadership and tactical skill to win victories and bedevil the

The red-robed Cardinal of Winchester relentlessly interrogated Joan in her cell while she was ill.

English? The short answer is, no one knows. Quite possibly, she simply displayed enough leadership qualities that the troops were willing to follow her and do her bidding.

★★★★★

IMPRISONMENT AND TRIAL

At Joan's trial, which began on 13 January 1431, this extraordinary military career was put on display. She was on trial as much for the fact that she wore men's armour and clothing, wielded a sword in combat, sat perfectly atop a horse in a man's war saddle and led men into combat, as for any perceived crime against religion.

During the trial, Joan was kept in a large tower of Rouen Castle. As she had made several escape attempts before she arrived in Rouen, she was placed in leg irons chained to a huge piece of wood. A squad of English soldiers guarded her twenty-four hours a day.

The trial itself consisted of repeated interrogations, many taking place in the royal chapel of the castle. From the beginning, the judges were confronted by a stubborn and determined individual. When asked to swear an oath to tell the truth, she replied: 'I do not know what you will ask me about. Perhaps you will ask me things which I shall not tell you.' (She finally agreed to take a very limited oath.)

After questioning her on her childhood and military matters, the examiners returned repeatedly to the subject of Joan's voices. She could not (or would not) quite say what the saints she claimed to have seen looked like (although she described Michael as being quite handsome), and became irritated when pushed on the subject: 'I have told you all I know about that and rather than tell you all I know I would prefer you cut off my head!'

★ ★ ★ ★ ★

RECANTATION AND EXECUTION

Though the judges continually set traps, Joan was proving no pushover; so much so that the embarrassed Bishop Cauchon decided to stop holding semi-public sessions of the trial. Still, the strain on Joan was enormous. Not yet twenty, without legal

Joan of Arc was taken by cart to the marketplace where her terrible death would be witnessed by a large crowd from all stations in life.

defenders or representation of any kind, she had only herself and her voices to rely on.

And, while the voices came to her in prison — indeed, during the trial itself — she sometimes said that they were inaudible or confusing.

I. PATROIS. 67.

Battered on all sides, faced with a horrible death by burning, she agreed to publicly renounce her voices. She did so on 24 May, in the town's cemetery, with an executioner's wagon nearby, ready to take her to be burned if she faltered. She was then sentenced to life imprisonment. She made her recantation wearing women's clothing, possibly to show that she was cooperating with the authorities.

However, Joan could not keep up this charade. By the following Sunday, once more wearing men's clothing, she announced that she was hearing her voices again.

The court sentenced her to be burned at the stake the following day. Despite the fact that Joan must have seen this coming, she was distraught on the morning of her death. 'Am I to be treated so horribly and cruelly that my body, which has never been corrupted, must today be consumed and reduced to ash. Ah! Ah! I would seven times rather be beheaded than to be thus burned', she cried out, and could not be comforted.

Just before 9 am on 30 May, Joan was placed in a cart and brought to the marketplace, surrounded by English guards. She was now, at this final moment, dressed in women's clothes — wearing a black shift with a black kerchief over her head, and she wept profusely. After a priest gave a sermon, a bishop's headdress was forced on her head and she was proclaimed a heretic and an idolater, a worshipper of false gods.

THE SOUND OF WHOSE VOICE?

Was Joan of Arc crazy? Some modern psychiatrists have diagnosed her with schizophrenia — certainly her voices and hallucinations fit into this pattern, and schizophrenia often begins in adolescence. But many historians have doubts about this, since Joan was actually able to function at a very high level, commanding men in battle and brilliantly parrying her questioners at her trial, something a schizophrenic would have difficulty doing.

Some experts have claimed that Joan's hallucinations may have resulted from organic causes — from mould spores, say, or a type of tuberculosis — but these explanations are not terribly convincing. We may just have to take Joan's word for it: that her voices were from God.

One priest accompanied Joan to the scaffold. As she was chained to the stake, it appeared that she had begun hearing her voices again; those nearby heard her call out to St Michael. She also exclaimed, 'Rouen, Rouen, shall I die here?' as if she could not believe her fate. She begged for a cross and one was shown to her.

Then the fire was lit. The huge noisy crowd fell into perfect silence as the Maid's shrieks and pleas rose up to the heavens. As the flames enveloped her, she began to cry out for holy water. Her suffering lasted a long time — the executioner later explained that the stake was placed so high up he could not reach the young woman to mercifully strangle her, as was customary in such cases. He was so moved by her plight that he wept. Yet by order of the authorities, he was ordered to rake the fire back after Joan died, so that the crowd could truly see that she was dead.

Then she was burned to ashes, and the ashes thrown into the Seine. All except her heart, which — according to a legend that sprang up — could not be burned at all.

COLUMBUS ARRIVES IN THE AMERICAS

[1492]

★ ★ ★ ★ ★ ★ ★ ★ ★ ★ ★ ★ ★ ★ ★

The search for a maritime trading route joins two worlds

In his journal Christopher Columbus records his departure: '[We] set sail on Friday, 3 August, half an hour before sunrise, steering for the Canary Islands ... thence to the Indies ...'. Columbus was setting off on a voyage that was the most important ever undertaken. Never before, or since, has such a vast discovery of unknown territory been made. It offered the continent of Europe a fertile new ground for nation-building. Within a few short years, Spain, France, England, Portugal and the Netherlands were involved in a fierce race to grab as much land in the newly discovered Americas as possible. It would permanently alter the balance of power in Europe.

For those who lived in the Americas, however, Columbus's landing would be a singular disaster. They would be decimated as much by European disease (such as smallpox) as by European steel, and their way of life would be completely destroyed.

Columbus kneels before Ferdinand II and Isabella, King and Queen of Spain, upon his return from the New World.

★ ★ ★ ★ ★

FINDING A WAY EAST

It wasn't as if the two worlds had never touched before, of course. The Chinese of ancient times may have travelled to Central America. The Vikings had crossed the Atlantic (at the time generally referred to as the 'Ocean Sea') numerous times, sailing to Labrador and Newfoundland in the years between 1000 and 1300 AD. But mostly these journeys were trips to pick up timber or find good fishing, and contact with this unknown world was not exploited.

Columbus's voyage came about because European countries, in particular Spain and Portugal, wanted to find a sea route to the 'Indies' (as India and China were known). These exotic destinations provided Europe with lucrative trading opportunities. Pioneering a route to the east from Europe that avoided the long and perilous overland journey through Central Asia could bring fabulous wealth.

The Portuguese were fabled mariners and had already led attempts to reach the Indies, heading east via Africa and the Cape of Good Hope. Attention now began to focus on the idea of reaching the East by sailing west. (Most people of learning by now accepted that the world was round.) Attempts had been made as early as the late thirteenth century — but the mariners never returned. It was a voyage, everyone agreed, that was fraught with extreme peril.

★ ★ ★ ★ ★

ROYAL APPROVAL

About forty years old at the time of his legendary voyage, Columbus was born in Genoa, Italy, a thriving city of seafarers and traders. He sailed the Mediterranean for various Italian city-states before going to work for the Portuguese and their king, John II.

Columbus proposed to King John that he should sail west, across the Western Sea, to the Indies. John rejected the proposal, so Columbus took his idea to Ferdinand and Isabella (or Ysabel

Born in the Italian city-state of Genoa, Columbus went to sea as a young boy and became a brilliant seaman and navigator.

in the Castillian spelling of the day), heads of a newly unified Spain. They agreed to back him.

Columbus was an odd figure. He was a loner, arrogant and ambitious, out to become 'Admiral of the Ocean Sea' (as he asked his sponsors to name him). Yet he was an undeniably brave and brilliant seaman. He knew from his extensive seafaring experience that two different wind systems operated in the Atlantic, forming a circulation. The north-east trade winds would push him across the ocean from the latitude of the Canary Islands, and the south-westerly trades, which blew further north, would push him in the opposite direction. The question was, would they be strong enough to get him back home?

Aided by strong trade winds, the Pinta, *the* Niña *and the* Santa María *sped swiftly towards their destination in the New World.*

SECRETLY MAKING HEADWAY

Setting sail, Columbus had with him three ships: the *Niña*, the *Pinta* and the *Santa María*; his crew consisted of ninety men. The ships were caravels, two- or three-masted sailing vessels. At the beginning of the ocean crossing, heading west from the Canary Islands, Columbus recorded nothing but good sailing weather — strong westerly winds, blue skies, and flying fish leaping through the air.

Columbus's crews carried provisions for a year, but he expected the voyage to take only a few weeks. The geographies he had consulted indicated that the Ocean Sea between Europe and the Indies was very narrow at the latitude Columbus was following. In the first ten days of his voyage, the trade winds sped him along for 1160 nautical miles (a nautical mile is 1.85 kilometres). On his best day, he made 174 nautical miles (322 kilometres).

This speed was a mixed blessing, however, for Columbus expected the outlying islands of the Indies to appear any day, and they did not. Concerned that his crew might begin to become fearful, he lied to them about the distance they had covered each day, always telling his men they had travelled a lesser distance.

★ ★ ★ ★ ★

BEWILDERED AND BECALMED

In the third week of September, Columbus's ships encountered an alarming phenomenon: the Sargasso Sea. Looking like a great meadow of yellow and green grass, the Sargasso is made up of sargassum, a thick weed and extends 1100 by 3200 kilometres in the mid-Atlantic near Bermuda. It is harmless to ships, but since no European had ever sailed through it before, the men did not know that.

Around this same time, the trade winds seemed to falter, and the ships were forced to sail much more slowly. They travelled only about 400 kilometres in five days, and the sea was so smooth the men were able to shout between vessels to each other, and dive off to go swimming. On 25 September, a lookout on the *Pinta* shouted 'Tierra! Tierra!' and everyone believed they saw a high mountain in the distance. Columbus even sank to his knees to thank God. But it turned out to be a mirage.

★ ★ ★ ★ ★

DESPAIR – THEN JOY

While Columbus recorded in his journal that 'the sea was like a river' and the air 'sweet and soft', the men were growing suspicious. To these sailors, Columbus was a foreigner, a Genoese, and not a very likeable one at that. As the ships moved further and further into the unknown, with no sight of land, they began to grumble openly.

In his desperation to find land, he ordered that the ships sail at night, a dangerous prospect in unknown waters if land is thought to be near. All hands therefore kept a sharp lookout. Around 2 am on 12 October, Rodrigo de Triana, lookout on the *Pinta*, saw a white-sand cliff or beach gleaming in the distance and cried out 'Tierra! Tierra!'

This time it was no false alarm. Columbus soon pulled alongside in the slower *Santa María* and marked the distance to this welcome apparition as about 10 kilometres. The ships tacked back and forth, waiting for dawn.

The voyage from the Canary Islands had taken five weeks. Steering through uncharted waters, using celestial navigation, and dead reckoning, Columbus had managed to find the optimal course to the Americas — a course that Spanish ships would follow for centuries to come.

★ ★ ★ ★ ★

A MOMENTOUS MEETING

Columbus had brought his men to an outlying island of the Bahamas. At daylight, they sailed to an opening in the reef and entered a shallow bay. They suddenly saw a group of naked people run down to the shore and stare in astonishment at the Spanish ships.

Columbus, with a group of armed men, rowed to shore. Columbus carried the royal banner, while others in the party carried flags bearing green crosses and the letters F and Y (the initials of the Spanish king and queen). Once on shore, they fell on their knees and praised God for their salvation. Ignoring the naked people approaching, Columbus took possession of the island in the name of Spain.

The islanders turned out to be friendly and gentle. Although they had never seen men like these or ships of such size, they showed no fear. They wore their hair cut into a fringe over their

WHERE DID COLUMBUS LAND?

Many historians believe that Watlings Island in the Bahamas fits the description of San Salvador, the island where Columbus first touched land in the Americas. It is the right size, occupies the right geographical position and has an inland lake, which was described by Columbus. But many other historians, including a team of experts hired by the National Geographic Society to make a five-year study, favour tiny Samana Cay. It has some of the same features as Watlings, and may also have lain more directly in Columbus's path. Still other historians feel that Samana is too small and too arid to have ever supported a settlement like the one Columbus described (though recent archaeological findings seem to indicate at least some habitation of Samana at the time of the voyage). The debate will continue, but for now Watlings appears to get the nod.

Pointing upwards, the chief addresses Columbus on the immortality of the soul. Columbus, however, was more interested in the gold jewellery the natives wore.

eyebrows and long down their backs, painted their bodies and their faces white, black or red and had skin colouring that was neither black nor white.

The Indians appeared to be poor, but one thing caught Columbus's interest: many of them had gold hanging from holes pierced in their ears or noses. Asking about this using hand signals, he thought they told him that the gold came from an island to the south, where there was a great king. So, after spending three days on the island he named San Salvador, Columbus decided to leave and seek this island. He took seven Indian men with him as guides, giving them no choice in the matter. Thus the template was set for the conquest of the Americas: enslaved Indians accompanying Europeans on a single-minded hunt for gold.

★ ★ ★ ★ ★

SHORT-LIVED GLORY, LASTING FAME

Columbus continued exploring the islands for three months, hoping to find gold and the fabled land of the Indies. He did succeed in finding gold — on the island of Hispaniola. In January of 1493, he sailed north, found the south-westerly trade winds, and headed back to Spain.

When he arrived back in Spain, Columbus was given honours beyond his wildest imaginings. He was awarded the rank of 'Admiral of the Ocean Sea' and made viceroy and governor of all the lands he had discovered. He was to make three more voyages to the Caribbean. Stubborn to the end, he never gave up insisting the Americas were the Indies, despite growing evidence to the contrary. Spain continued to reap the benefits of Columbus's momentous discovery, and became a pre-eminent power in Europe.

Columbus had not found the Indies, nor had he really found a 'new' world. Instead, as the historian John H. Parry has put it, he 'established contact between two worlds, both already old'. But from that moment of contact, the modern world — one of extraordinary interchanges between far-flung cultures, both for good and ill — has sprung.

The mob, armed and dangerous, is ready to storm the Bastille.

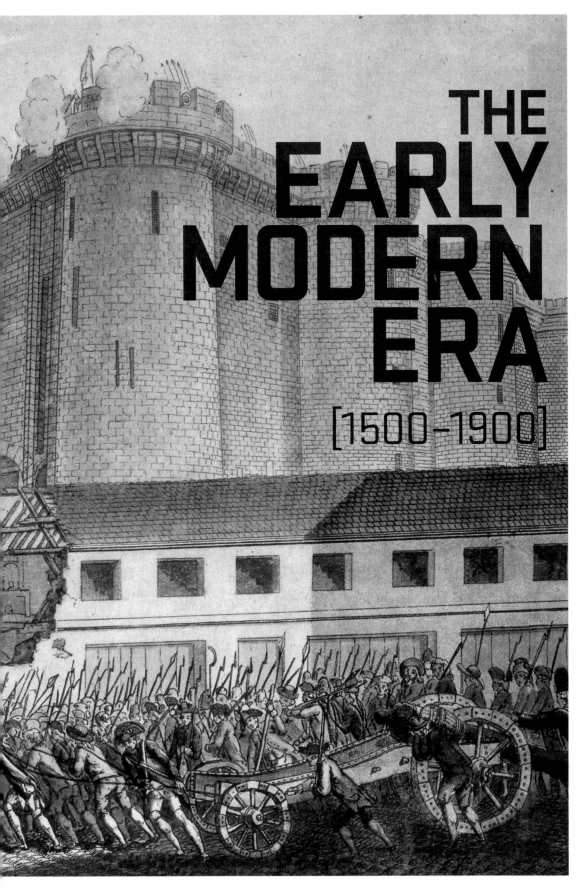

THE EARLY MODERN ERA

[1500–1900]

THE DEFEAT OF THE SPANISH ARMADA

[1588]

★ ★ ★ ★ ★ ★ ★ ★ ★ ★ ★ ★ ★ ★ ★

The sea battle that saved England, sparked the nation's long rise to maritime supremacy and rewrote the rules of naval combat

On the morning of 29 July, a guard spotted the dark shapes of dozens of ships far out over the waters of the English Channel. Within minutes, torches were touched to piles of resin-soaked brush that stood at the ready. Soon, a glowing necklace of fire lit up the southern English coastline, all the way from Cornwall to Plymouth, in whose harbour lay the English fleet. The fires were an alarm call, warning of the approach of the Spanish Armada. The great invasion fleet had been expected for some time. It posed the most serious threat their nation had faced for centuries.

The Spanish could see the glow of the fires. It soon became apparent to them that the English fleet, led by the Lord Admiral, Charles Howard, Second Baron Howard of Effingham, and his famous second-in-command, Sir Francis Drake, was coming to make a fight of it.

The Spanish Armada was the most potent invasion force that had ever threatened England.

The naval battle that followed would become a part of English folklore — it has long been recounted how Drake calmly continued his game of bowls after hearing the news of the Armada's approach. The battle enhanced England's status as a first-class naval power. It also marked a major shift in naval strategy, away from close-in fighting to the use of accurate, long-range cannon fire.

★ ★ ★ ★ ★

DEEP DIVISIONS

Long-standing differences and a succession of disputes led to this extraordinary battle between England and Spain. In a sense, the countries and their differences were embodied by their two rulers — Elizabeth I of England and King Philip II of Spain. The two monarchs and their countries had become enemies. This was partly the result of religious differences (Elizabeth was Protestant, Philip a Roman Catholic) and partly because England had begun to flex its muscles, particularly at sea. This put it at odds with Spain, then the most powerful seagoing nation in Europe.

★ ★ ★ ★ ★

NO ORDINARY FLEET

The huge Spanish fleet that entered the Channel on 29 July was 125 ships and 30,000 men strong. About twenty-five of the ships were mighty fighting galleons, the rest armed merchantmen, transport ships and pinnacles for swift scouting and message-bearing between the larger ships. The Armada was commanded by the Duke of Medina-Sidonia aboard his flagship, the *San Martín de Portugal*.

The English fleet was much lighter and more nimble and contained thirty-four royal warships and almost 200 other vessels. But although the English fleet was sizeable, it was

Sir Francis Drake also had a reputation as a pirate — raiding Spanish holdings in the Pacific and the West Indies.

in a desperate position. For the Armada was the most potent invasion force that had ever been pointed at England. Of its 30,000 men, only 7000 were sailors; the rest were soldiers. The ships contained powerful land artillery, siege equipment, six months' worth of food and wine, and tons of ammunition. The immediate objective of the Armada was not to fight the English fleet. Instead, it intended to head north and rendezvous with a second Spanish force in the Netherlands.

★ ★ ★ ★ ★

'GOD'S OBVIOUS DESIGN'

The Netherlands was to provide the flashpoint in the feud between Philip and Elizabeth. It had been under Spanish rule for some time, and the Dutch Protestants there had been persecuted for their religion. Any revolt against the Spanish was dealt with harshly. In 1587, religious and political tension increased when Elizabeth (fearing a plot against her) ordered the execution of the Catholic Mary Queen of Scots. In her will, Mary left her accession rights to the English throne to Philip (formerly her brother-in-law). Philip believed that the security of Spain depended on restoring a Catholic monarch to the throne of England. Of course, this meant the destruction of Elizabeth's Protestant regime. Even the pope agreed. It was, as one Spanish noble put it, 'God's obvious design' that Spain rule England.

★ ★ ★ ★ ★

PACKING FOR AN INVASION

The invasion strategy had been cobbled together from two separate plans. One plan was to make a surprise assault across the Channel. The alternative plan was to take a huge invasion force from Spain to land in England or possibly southern Ireland.

It was Philip who decided to merge the two plans. The Armada was to sail up the Channel with part of the invasion force. When it reached Flanders, it would protect the men as they crossed the Channel to Kent, and then unload its own forces. In total, some 50,000 well-provisioned Spanish troops would then find themselves ashore in England. Many in Philip's court envisioned a slaughter of the English.

For their part, the English knew that if they did not stop the Armada before it reached the Netherlands, an invasion of England would almost certainly occur.

★★★★★

NEW RULES OF BATTLE

The English attacked the Spanish fleet at about nine o'clock in the morning of 31 July, just off Plymouth. Divided into two groups, they struck at the flanks of the Spanish in single file, discharging their cannon at long distance.

> **FOR THEIR PART, THE ENGLISH KNEW THAT IF THEY DID NOT STOP THE ARMADA BEFORE IT REACHED THE NETHERLANDS, AN INVASION OF ENGLAND WOULD ALMOST CERTAINLY OCCUR.**

This cannonade may be thought of as the opening blow of modern naval warfare. With traditional naval warfare, ships tried to get close to each other. They would attach themselves to the enemy with grappling hooks, and fight what were essentially mini-infantry battles at sea. But the English had recently overhauled their strategy. They tailored their ships to move

BOWLING WHILE THE ARMADA APPROACHES?

Was Sir Francis Drake playing the English game of lawn bowls in Plymouth on the afternoon of 29 July when he heard of the news of the approaching Spanish Armada, as has long been reported? And did he say, 'We have time enough to finish the game and beat the Spaniards, too?'

Possibly, although not probably. Drake did like to bowl, as did most English gentlemen at the time, and Plymouth Hoe, the grassy open space by Plymouth Harbour, was perfect for the game. Such a statement also sounds like something that Drake, who was renowned for his impulsive behaviour and lack of reverence, might have said. But no one reported the statement at the time (the first record of it comes forty years later).

In any event, every English seaman present that day knew that the unfavourable tides would prevent the royal fleet leaving Plymouth Harbour until about ten o'clock at night. That left plenty of time for several games of bowls, not just one. So, if Drake did utter his famous statement, he was not being boastful. His comment simply reflected the reality of navigating against an ebb tide.

fast, and so avoid being boarded. Importantly, they discharged their cannon with improved accuracy. An English innovation helped greatly here — by replacing fixed gun mountings with movable carriages, cannon could be reloaded more rapidly. On 31 July, however, the cannonading had little effect initially. The English were perhaps overawed by what must have looked like an extraordinary metropolis of ships, a veritable city on the sea.

On 6 August, after a week of running battle, Medina-Sidonia anchored his fleet off Calais, the nearest French port to England. He waited for word from the Duke of Parma that he was ready to invade. The English, who were nearly out of ammunition, waited offshore, plotting their next move.

★ ★ ★ ★ ★

FLUSHING OUT THE ENEMY

Unfortunately, the Duke of Parma had been slow in putting together his own invasion force, and his 20,000 men were now being blockaded in their ports by Dutch rebels. To make matters darker for the Spanish, the water along the Flanders coast was shallow. This meant the deeper-draught Armada vessels could not strike close enough to shore to break the blockade.

Around midnight on 7–8 August, the English sent eight fire ships into the anchored Spanish fleet. These vessels were not just drifting old pinnacles filled with pitch and tar, but warships running at full sail, holds full of gunpowder, ready to be set alight by their suicidally courageous crews, who leaped off at the last possible moment. Two of the English fire ships penetrated the Spanish defences, wreaking havoc. The Spanish ships were forced to cut their anchor cables to escape and move to the open ocean — exactly where the English wanted them.

THE BATTLE OF GRAVELINES

On 9 August, the English closed in for a pitched, decisive battle off Gravelines, a town in the far south-west of the Spanish Netherlands. The engagement lasted eight hours, with English and Spanish ships engaged in ferocious cannon duels. Finally, the effect of the cannonading took its toll on the confused and

The Armada, *by Nicholas Hilliard, captures the drama of the fabled sea battle in which England emerged as the pre-eminent world naval power.*

scattered Spanish fleet. Four vessels were lost to English gunfire and the entire fleet was very nearly stranded on the sandbanks off Flanders.

When the wind turned to the west, pushing the ships off the sandbanks, Medina-Sidonia was faced with a choice. He could cross to invade England on his own and return south through the Channel — or head north and west, around the British Isles. With the prevailing winds against him, he chose this last course. Unfortunately for the Spanish, he did not know two things: one, Howard's English fleet was out of ammunition and could not have withstood a Spanish attack; and, two, horrible gales would assault the Spanish on the west coasts of Ireland and Scotland.

UNFORTUNATELY FOR THE SPANISH, HE DID NOT KNOW TWO THINGS: ONE, HOWARD'S ENGLISH FLEET WAS OUT OF AMMUNITION AND COULD NOT HAVE WITHSTOOD A SPANISH ATTACK; AND, TWO, HORRIBLE GALES WOULD ASSAULT THE SPANISH ON THE WEST COASTS OF IRELAND AND SCOTLAND.

During the long return voyage, thousands of Spanish sailors drowned in storms, and hundreds were killed by scavengers along the British coastlines. By the time it returned to Spain, the Armada had lost about half its invasion fleet, as well as 14,000 soldiers and seamen. During the battle, the English had lost only seven ships.

★ ★ ★ ★ ★

A PATRIOTIC MYTH

In the short run, the victory saved England from a Spanish invasion and a Roman Catholic monarch on its throne. It also helped preserve an independent Netherlands. Of the two royal adversaries, Elizabeth was to live longer, until 1604, while Philip, blinded by cataracts and with a crippled arm (probably from a stroke), died in 1598.

Eventually, the defeat of the Spanish Armada was seen as marking the beginning of English supremacy over the seas, which reached its full fruition after Admiral Lord Nelson's victory over the French at Trafalgar in 1805. It is also seen as the demise of Spain as a great naval power, though more recently historians have concluded that this demise did not begin until the middle of the next century.

Regardless of this, victory over the Spanish Armada provided the English with an enduring patriotic myth — much like the French storming of the Bastille — that would be summoned back into the public consciousness again and again when the country faced dark days in the future.

THE STORMING OF THE BASTILLE

★ ★ ★ ★ ★ ★ ★ ★ ★ ★ ★ ★ ★ ★ ★ ★

The downfall of a notorious symbol of tyranny triggers a momentous revolution

The storming of the Bastille on 14 July 1789 is renowned and celebrated as the heroic uprising that kick-started the French Revolution. An infamous symbol of oppression was conquered and many of the French Crown's most hard-done-by and mistreated victims were liberated. But as with many legends of the French Revolution and other uprisings in history, the reality was somewhat different. Nothing highlights this better than the scenes that immediately followed the liberation.

When the mob broke through the gates of the infamous fourteenth century jail, the prison was discovered to be almost empty. Unknown to the attackers, the government had scheduled the building for demolition and only six prisoners were left in all of its many cells and chambers. Four of the prisoners were forgers. Two were insane. One of these was a deranged Irishman known to history only as Major Whyte.

With the storming of the Bastille, a motley group of prisoners is freed from its dungeons.

★ ★ ★ ★ ★

INEVITABLE BUT UNFORESEEN

According to one commentator, writing almost half a century later, the French Revolution was both 'inevitable yet ... completely unforeseen'. The Revolution arose in a France wracked by extreme poverty, and would change the face, not only of France, but of Europe. When the revolutionaries came to power, established a constitutional democracy and executed France's formerly untouchable monarchs, shock waves spread through nearby nations. They feared such progressive ideas might be exported to their own countries. And not just ideas. As the French Revolution went careening out of control, with thousands of nobles and alleged counter-revolutionaries executed, it seemed to observers that violent bloodshed would be inevitable.

However, the French Revolution, like most revolutions, began out of a genuine desire to reduce hunger and injustice.

★ ★ ★ ★ ★

'RAVENOUS SCARECROWS'

In the early spring of 1789, France, a country of about twenty-six million people, suffered from a level of poverty that horrified even hardened foreign observers. One English writer described seeing everywhere starving peasants who looked like 'ravenous scarecrows'. There were numerous reasons for this level of poverty, but heavy taxes were chief among them. These taxes were almost universally borne by the peasants and poor urban workers, rather than by nobles or the rich and powerful Catholic Church. The taxes were particularly burdensome in the city of Paris. Every foodstuff, dried good, barrel of wine, or mooing, baaing, clucking head of livestock coming into the city for sale was stopped at a 'customs barrier' and its owner forced to pay an excise tax.

With a staggering national debt, France was in terrible shape. King Louis XVI had inherited this situation but had been unable to do much about it. Although not the beast he was later made out to be, he was an uncertain king. He seemed to display little sympathy for the needs of the common people.

Prior to 1789, France already had an assembly (a kind of parliament) — made up of the First Estate (the clergy), the Second Estate (the aristocracy) and the Third Estate (the middle class and the peasants) — but it hadn't met since 1614. Under pressure, Louis XVI called the assembly together to deal with the crisis of the worsening economy and starving peasantry.

FIERY DEBATES TOOK PLACE ON STREET CORNERS AND ORDINARY PEOPLE BEGAN TO SENSE THAT THEY NOW MIGHT HAVE A SAY IN THEIR OWN FUTURES.

The clergy and nobility stifled the Third Estate's demands for reform. Led by a group of radical Parisians, the Third Estate broke off and formed a new body, the National Assembly, whose purpose was to create a French constitution. An increasingly powerless Louis was forced to accept this development.

Soon, liberty was in the air in Paris. Fiery debates took place on street corners and ordinary people — merchants, students, farmers from the countryside — began to sense that they now might have a say in their own futures.

★ ★ ★ ★ ★

CITIZENS TAKE UP ARMS

The incident that sparked the storming of the Bastille was the dismissal of Jacques Necker, Louis XVI's finance minister. The king's conservative advisers had urged him to fire Necker, who had shown sympathy for the plight of the French people and had approved of the formation of the National Assembly. Louis did so on 11 July. By 13 July, crowds were demonstrating in protest in the streets of central Paris.

Rumours spread that Louis was about to unleash his Swiss and German mercenaries on the crowd, since his own French-born army could not be trusted to fire on their fellow citizens. Inflamed by this and intoxicated with the sudden feel of freedom in the air, the demonstrators — the citizens' army, as they called themselves — became desperate for arms to defend themselves. Shortly after dawn on Tuesday 14 July, they broke into the basement of the Hôtel des Invalides, a military complex and hospital, and took over 28,000 muskets and ten cannon. The only problem was they had very little powder and ball with which to fire their weapons. Fearing that the ammunition might be used by the rebels, the commander of the Invalides had sent it to be stored protectively in the stark fortress of the Bastille — all 9000 kilograms of it.

To the mob, the Bastille was not only a source of powder and ball, it was also a symbol of the long-standing political and social system dominated by the aristocracy. An enormous building with eight rounded towers and walls 25 metres high, the Bastille (from a French word meaning 'castle' or 'fortress') had first been a military stronghold. It was later used as a state prison. It had more recently gained a sinister reputation as a place that housed those who had committed political crimes, real or imagined, against the Crown.

★ ★ ★ ★ ★

THE NERVOUS GOVERNOR

The governor of the Bastille was the Marquis de Launay. Forces defending the prison amounted to eighty-two pensioned-off soldiers, or *invalides*, reinforced however by a command of thirty-two professional Swiss soldiers and thirty or so cannon. Many were aimed right at the crowd now approaching.

A massive burden of crippling taxation was carried by the peasants and the urban poor. The nobility and clergy paid no taxes.

The thick gate to the inner courtyard of the prison lay across a drawbridge over a dry moat. Once through that, any attackers would have to brave still another moat and drawbridge before arriving in the Bastille proper.

In an attempt to avert confrontation, certain members of the new National Assembly raced ahead of the mob to speak with Launay, at about ten o'clock in the morning. They asked him to withdraw the guns, which he did. While these negotiations were going on, however, a crowd of about a thousand arrived outside the walls of the Bastille, crying 'We want [the] Bastille! Out with the troops!'

Impatient with the pace of the negotiations going on inside the prison, a few of the demonstrators gained entrance to the inner courtyard. There, they grabbed sledgehammers and smashed the chains holding the drawbridge up. It came

DEMOLISHING THE BASTILLE

The Bastille did not long survive. It at once became an attraction for visitors hoping to see some signs of the horrors of bygone days (a few old bones and some chains were produced, but by and large nothing grotesque was found within the old fortress's walls). Then, in 1790, a French entrepreneur and showman named Pierre-François Palloy won the rights to demolish the structure, so that he could sell pieces of it to eager souvenir hunters. Palloy personally knocked the first stone off with a pickaxe. Demolition then continued, involving as many as a thousand workers, and was finished by November. As well as selling off much of the structure, Palloy created a masonry model of the prison and held festivals amid the ruins. Today, the former site of the prison is occupied by a broad square, the Place de la Bastille, and the Bastille Opera.

crashing down across the moat — killing one rioter who could not get out of the way in time — and the mob surged into the inner courtyard.

At this point, at about 2 pm, someone opened fire. (Who was responsible has never been determined.) In any event, bullets and cannon shot began to fly, as the demonstrators scattered to the side of the courtyard. Makeshift pallets carrying the wounded began to emerge onto the streets from the smoky courtyards.

Inside, Launay was frantic. Despite there being numerous French troops stationed nearby, none had come to his aid — both because many within the ranks of the infantry sympathised with the rebels and because central Paris had been virtually abandoned to the mob.

★ ★ ★ ★ ★

THE FORTRESS FALLS

Finally, reinforcements came — but not to Launay. At about 3.30 pm, the mob was joined by a few hundred *gardes français*, soldiers of the rebellion's 'new militia', formed from any man or woman who could acquire a gun, as well as deserters from Louis XVI's forces.

Led by two veteran officers, the militia members set up the guns in the inner courtyard, aiming them directly at the wooden bottom of the raised drawbridge (the walls of the prison were too thick for cannon shot to penetrate). On the other side of the gate, Launay lined up his own cannon. Perhaps 30 metres apart, the forces of old and new faced each other.

Shortly thereafter, after failed negotiations, Launay gave up without condition. The drawbridge was opened and the mob poured into the Bastille.

A SYMBOL OF FREEDOM

The rebels disarmed the Swiss soldiers and led them through the streets, stoning them and screaming at them. The soldiers survived, however, unlike some of the *invalides*, who were mistaken for prison wardens and hung or beaten to death. Launay, too, suffered a horrible fate when the mob stabbed and shot him to death and then carved off his head to put on a pike.

Eighty-three members of the mob died, but the victory of the crowd was great. On the evening after the fall of the prison, huge crowds thronged Paris, shouting, celebrating and firing their guns in the air.

The king announced that he would approve a new government. However, many nobles were appalled at the violence (which would later claim the king's life, as well as that of his wife, Marie Antoinette), and began fleeing the country.

During the next decade, France would be radically transformed. More widespread mob violence would turn the Revolution very ugly, very soon. During the Reign of Terror, which began in 1792, thousands of those suspected of 'counter-revolutionary' sympathies were killed. This terror was to forever tarnish the ideals of the Revolution.

But on 14 July 1789, it was truly the common people who took the first step towards a republic. And ever since, Bastille Day has been celebrated annually in France as the day when the people, at least symbolically speaking, won their freedom.

Bullets and cannon balls began to fly, the air filled with smoke, as demonstrators surged towards the entrance of the Bastille.

THE BATTLE OF WATERLOO

[1815]

★ ★ ★ ★ ★ ★ ★ ★ ★ ★ ★ ★ ★ ★ ★

How Napoleon finally met his match, and Europe turned its back on revolution

It's just possible that the Battle of Waterloo is the most famous battle in the history of the world. Sure, it has a few strong competitors. But Waterloo is one of the very few battles in world history that decided the outcome of a war on a single day. The mighty clash at Waterloo also encouraged war planners for years to come to plot massive set-piece battles that might end conflicts at a single, bold stroke. It was this belief that was to cause much carnage when World War I began.

To this day, the very name of the battle is associated with crushing defeat and personal downfall. But, in Belgium, on that June day of 1815, things could have gone quite differently.

★ ★ ★ ★ ★

As one of the most famous battles in history, the Battle of Waterloo has been the subject of many paintings.

A QUIET MORNING

On the morning of 18 June 1815, a few kilometres outside the Belgian village of Waterloo, 140,000 men faced each other over a piece of land 3 kilometres wide and about 1 kilometre across.

On the north side, drawn up along and behind a ridge, was the Army of the Seventh Coalition. The army contained forces from Great Britain, the Netherlands, Belgium and Germany, totalling about 67,000 men.

Their commander was the Duke of Wellington, the most successful British general of his generation. An allied Prussian army under Field Marshal Gebhard von Blücher was not far away. To the south across the field were 73,000 French troops commanded by Napoleon Bonaparte.

It had rained heavily and both armies had spent the night in the fields, miserable and cold. The open land separating the two armies had become a morass of mud. After dawn, the skies cleared and the sun came out. The British readied themselves, certain that the notably aggressive Napoleon would attack their positions, and then … nothing happened.

This was unlike Napoleon. Those who knew him had never seen him slowed by inconveniences like muddy fields. And the longer the delay, the greater chance that von Blücher's Prussian forces would reach Wellington in time to back up his troops — the very thing Napoleon wanted to avoid. Many in the French ranks began to ask, what was the matter with the emperor?

★ ★ ★ ★ ★

THE THREAT TO EUROPE

This confrontation in Belgium was a final showdown after almost two decades of conflict in Europe. After the French Revolution in 1789, France was at war with most of Europe. Napoleon seized power in France in 1799 and appointed himself emperor in 1804. As he set out to seize more territory, hostilities with his European neighbours intensified.

When Napoleon was forced to abdicate after his disastrous attack on Russia, he went into exile. Louis XVIII was restored to power. The Coalition powers supported this move as they

After an outstanding military career, Arthur Wellesley, First Duke of Wellington, served two short terms as British Prime Minister.

wanted a stable monarchy in France. Europe breathed a sigh of relief, and most of the armies disbanded.

But not for long.

After escaping from Elba on 26 February 1815, Napoleon landed in France, where he was met by a regiment of soldiers. They had been sent by Louis XVIII to capture or kill him. Yet the soldiers spontaneously rallied in support of Napoleon and marched on Paris with him. Louis XVIII fled, and Napoleon, using the same charisma that had brought the Fifth Regiment to his side, raised an army that consisted of many of his old imperial soldiers.

It was a time of enormous concern for the Coalition powers in Europe. Here was a man many considered a dangerous megalomaniac, returned from what was supposed to be permanent exile. With astonishing swiftness, he had raised an army of 73,000 men. He needed to be stopped, and immediately, or the very future of Europe was at risk.

ESCAPE FROM ELBA

In 1814, Napoleon was exiled by Coalition powers to the island of Elba, off the coast of Italy. He was not, literally, a prisoner. He had a personal guard of six hundred or so men, was ruler of Elba's population of around 120,000 and was also allowed, perhaps cruelly, to keep the title of 'Emperor'. British ships guarded the island around the clock, but, even so, Napoleon was not isolated from the outside world and received thousands of letters from supporters all over Europe, which stoked his still simmering ambitions. On 26 February 1815, around midnight, he was fairly easily able to board a ship, elude the British vessels guarding Elba, and then make his way to France, and eventually to Waterloo.

Britain, Austria, Prussia and Russia responded quickly when the news came that Napoleon had escaped. They assembled another Coalition — the seventh to fight Napoleon — and declared war on France on 25 March. The intention was to surround France on all sides, march on Paris, and destroy Napoleon once and for all. But the only force ready to fight was Wellington's Anglo-allied army in Belgium, although the Prussian force commanded by von Blücher would soon be on its way to join the British commander.

Napoleon, meanwhile, deployed his army along the French border and sent Marshal Ney to attack the Prussians. After fierce fighting, the French forced von Blücher's army to retreat and Napoleon brought his army, on the evening of 17 June, to the village of Waterloo.

★ ★ ★ ★ ★

PAINFULLY AFFLICTED

Forty-five years old as the engagement began (just a few months younger than the Duke of Wellington), Napoleon was in an odd state of indecision on the morning of the battle. He arose quite early, and conferred with his generals over maps.

After reviewing his troops, he did not give any order to attack, giving as his only excuse the fact that the ground was still too muddy to manoeuvre. Finally, he asked his aides to take him to a small inn at the rear of the lines, where he dismounted his horse and sat on a chair, at one point putting his elbows on his knees and placing his face in his hands.

Years after Napoleon's death, both his brother and his personal physician revealed that the emperor suffered fiercely from an affliction he found embarrassing to admit to — haemorrhoids, which if aggravated by long periods of sitting on a hard surface, such as a saddle, became particularly painful. He may also have been suffering from other afflictions, including a pituitary disorder that led to weight gain as well as indecisiveness and blurry thinking. Whatever was happening, it wasn't until around 11.30 am that Napoleon roused himself from his lethargy and ordered that the attack begin with a cannonade.

★ ★ ★ ★ ★

THE THUNDER OF ARTILLERY

The relief among Coalition troops that the action was finally underway turned to horror, as French cannonballs weighing four and 6 kilograms flew through their ranks, wreaking havoc. One raw British recruit watched his sergeant major literally cut in half by a ball.

At this point, the Duke of Wellington's foresight came into play. He had chosen a ridge amid the farmers' fields near Waterloo as a place to make a stand against the French. Its reverse slope would offer protection against the French artillery assault. Although the artillery assault was to be the worst many a veteran soldier could remember, most of the cannonballs flew over the men and landed well to the rear. When the barrage ended, after perhaps half an hour, the Coalition infantry raised their heads.

★ ★ ★ ★ ★

HALTING THE CHARGE

When the Coalition forces rushed to reoccupy their lines at the centre of the ridge, they saw, coming directly at their left centre, three columns of French infantry, each twenty-four ranks deep and 150 soldiers wide. These were flanked by cavalry on either side. This was the classic and deadly formation of the French Grand Army.

The French soldiers marched, as one British officer said admiringly, 'as if on parade', directly at the Belgian division.

Unnerved, the Belgians turned and ran, leaving a great hole in the centre of the Coalition lines. But all was not as it seemed in the French ranks: amid the deafening noise soldiers could not hear their leaders' commands.

THE COMBAT SOON TURNED INTO HUNDREDS OF DEADLY HAND-TO-HAND BATTLES IN THE SWIRLING SMOKE, FOUGHT WITH RIFLE BUTT, SABRE, PIKE AND FISTS.

When the Scots poured a volley from 3000 rifles into the French columns at close range, the French outnumbered the Scots many times over. But because of their column formation they could not bring as many rifles to bear in reply. The combat soon turned into hundreds of deadly hand-to-hand battles in the swirling smoke, fought with rifle butt, sabre, pike and fists. Then, there came an amazing sight: leaping the hedges, as if in a steeplechase, the British cavalry arrived, led by the Scots Greys, in a charge that utterly destroyed the French advance.

★ ★ ★ ★ ★

ON THE RUN

Heavy fighting now raged around three isolated farmhouses and their outbuildings, ready-made defensive positions. After a bloody fight, the French infantry managed to seize one of the buildings from British hands. French artillery was then put into position there, aiming directly at the Coalition-held ridge. But when backup was requested, Napoleon said he had none to spare. When the Prussian forces under von Blücher arrived, Napoleon was appalled. His commander, the Marquis

The Battle of Waterloo raged all day, descending into bloody hand-to-hand fighting.

de Grouchy, had failed to block these troops, and von Blücher made his way to Wellington.

Napoleon sent one last roaring attack of his elite forces, the Imperial Guard, against the Coalition-held ridge. But while some managed to break through, the rest were overwhelmed and began to flee. Seeing this elite corps on the run, the French lines broke, pursued by the Coalition cavalry. Napoleon's army was now in flight and Napoleon himself, bitter, broken and ill, retreated with it to Paris.

★ ★ ★ ★ ★

FINAL EXILE

On the battlefield that night lay 40,000 men, dead or horribly wounded. The subsequent looting has passed into legend. Ghoulish Belgian peasants stripped thousands of dead men bare, while Coalition soldiers wandered through the night, sometimes even robbing and killing their own.

The very next day, Belgian civilian sightseers came out to wander the battlefield, holding handkerchiefs over their noses against the unpleasant smell. They knew that Napoleon had finally been defeated here, this time for good, and that therefore history had been made.

Forced to surrender on 15 July, the ailing general was exiled once again, this time to the tiny South Atlantic island of St Helena. Here he was to die in 1821, possibly poisoned, possibly, finally, a victim of the many ailments that had begun to plague him at Waterloo.

Europe had been saved, but the political effects of the Battle of Waterloo would be long lasting. Europe's leading powers became fiercely conservative and would resist change. Nationalist and republican movements were quashed.

Supporters of the old order well knew how close they had come to catastrophe. As the Duke of Wellington said of the Battle of Waterloo itself, it was 'the nearest-run thing you ever saw in your life'.

THE IRISH POTATO FAMINE

[1845–1849]

How nineteenth century Europe's greatest disaster accelerated one of the largest emigration movements in history and fuelled the rise of Irish nationalism

During the cool, wet summer of 1846, those Irish peasants who had managed to stave off starvation waited anxiously for their potato crops to come in. Surely the potato would not fail again, would not turn black and stinking on its vine, as it had done the previous year.

At first, the crop seemed healthy, but by September, potatoes began to die in the west of Ireland. Then, the malevolent disease moved across the country, at a rate of 80 kilometres a week, until no potato remained untouched. With only enough potatoes left in Ireland to feed people for one month, Black '47 was about to begin.

In this bleak image, an Irish peasant girl guards her family's last few possessions after eviction for non-payment of rent.

A DRAMATIC IMPACT

The following statistics convey the magnitude of the impact of the Great Hunger on Irish history. In 1845, the population of Ireland was about eight million. Six years later, it was five and a half million. About one million had died of starvation and disease. The other million and a half had emigrated — mainly to Britain, Australia and America.

The effect of this population loss was extreme. It left Ireland an impoverished country for generations to come. It also began the rise to prominence of Irish communities in countries around the world, most notably the United States and Australia.

★ ★ ★ ★ ★

KING POTATO

As the Irish consumed their last supplies of potatoes and the winter of 1846–47 began, they started to eat nettles, turnips, rotten cabbages, seaweed, even grass.

Few countries were as vulnerable to famine as Ireland. It had been dependent on the single crop of the potato since the 1590s, when it was imported from South America. In the cool, wet climate of Ireland, this marvellous life-giving tuber thrived. With little labour, one acre (0.4 hectares) of the very scarce farmland in Ireland could bring up to 11 tonnes of potatoes a year, enough to feed a large Irish family easily.

It has been estimated that by the mid-nineteenth century three million Irish survived on potatoes alone, with perhaps a little cabbage and buttermilk added. One adult Irish person would generally eat up to 6 kilograms of potatoes a day. Potatoes were rich in protein, carbohydrates and vitamin C — if poverty forces you to eat just one food, the potato is not the worst choice you can make.

Unfortunately, not only did the Irish cultivate only one food source, but they grew only one variety of potato, called Lumpers. It produced a high yield but was vulnerable to being completely destroyed by blights. Because it was not genetically diverse, a single blight could wipe it out.

The cause of the blight was a killer fungus called *Phytophthora infestans*. It had been brought from America on ships to England, and then blown by the wind across the Irish Sea. This fungus not only killed the potatoes, it turned them black and rotten, leaving them putrefying in their beds. What's more, it returned with a vengeance the following year.

During the winter of 1846–47, the worst anyone could remember, people began pouring into government poorhouses. These places were hellholes, rife with disease and desperation. In one poorhouse in Cork, fifty per cent of the children admitted in late 1846 died. The chief magistrate, a man named Nicholas Cummins, wrote in horror of a visit to one poorhouse: 'Six

THIS FUNGUS NOT ONLY KILLED THE POTATOES, IT TURNED THEM BLACK AND ROTTEN, LEAVING THEM PUTREFYING IN THEIR BEDS.

famished and ghastly skeletons to all appearances dead were huddled in a corner on some filthy straw ... I approached with horror and found by a low moaning that they were still alive. They were in fever ... in a few minutes I was surrounded by at least two hundred such phantoms ... Their demoniacal yells are still ringing in my ear ...' Stories like this had been coming out of Ireland for a year — and now people were dying, truly, by the thousands. Why wasn't anyone doing anything about it?

'THE ENGLISH GAVE US THE FAMINE'

The Irish had been fighting the English occupiers of their country on and off for two centuries before the famine. The *1801 Act of Union* integrated Ireland into Great Britain, yet the Irish were still considered poor cousins. Catholic Ireland remained under the control of an Anglo-Protestant landlord class that owned vast tracts of land. Most of these British landlords seldom visited their holdings, which were divided into tiny parcels and sublet to tenant farmers. It has been estimated that perhaps 400,000 Irish peasants lived on plots of 2 hectares or smaller.

There is a saying among the Irish that 'God gave us the potato blight, but the English gave us the famine'. When the famine first hit, the British Prime Minister Sir Robert Peel tried to help those in need by removing the duties on imported corn, paying for Indian corn (maize) to be imported to feed the hungry, and setting up other relief efforts. But even this mild and inadequate response met with opposition in Britain, and Peel was voted out of office in the summer of 1846.

★ ★ ★ ★ ★

A CRUEL AND BIGOTED RESPONSE

With the demise of Peel, control of the Irish was left entirely up to the Assistant Secretary of the British Treasury, Charles Edward Trevelyan. He visited Ireland only once during the famine. He claimed that, unlike the majority of those who witnessed the suffering at first-hand, he was unmoved by the experience — and that this made him better able to make decisions. One of his first was to halt shipments of government food, for fear that the Irish would become 'habitually dependent'. The only option left to the bulk of famine victims was public works relief. In the winter of 1846–47, 700,000 Irish — men, women and children — found work breaking stones with hammers, transporting the pieces in baskets and laying roads. But the pay was so poor they couldn't afford enough food to ease their hunger; and so, in turn, the people grew too weak for such hard labour.

Tens of thousands of tenants were evicted from their homes during the famine.

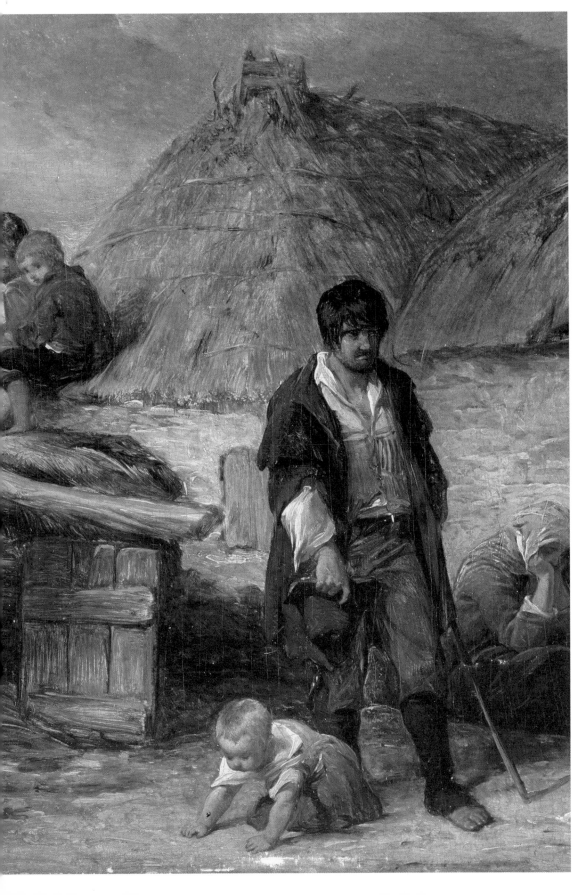

As 1847 wore on, villages were depopulated, with survivors too weak to bury the dead, who lay on the roadways. There were reports of cannibalism. There were outbreaks of typhus, dysentery and something called famine dropsy, which causes the limbs and the body to swell, and ends with the victim dropping dead suddenly. And the situation didn't just affect the peasantry: over 200 Irish doctors died in 1847 alone.

★ ★ ★ ★ ★

SUCCESS STORIES – AND LASTING SCARS

One and a half million Irish emigrated during the course of the Great Famine. They became workers, policemen and politicians in the United States, and gold miners, farmers and judges in Australia, most notably in Victoria, where one out of every four people by 1871 was an Irish immigrant. It was not an easy transition. The Irish who arrived in other countries were in sorry shape. They were malnourished, illiterate, usually toothless (as a result of scurvy or starvation) at very young ages, and more often than not disease-ridden. And something else distinguished them from other immigrants. Customs officials in Liverpool, from where many Irish emigrated, used adjectives like 'passive', 'resigned', 'stunned' and 'mute' to describe them in official records. Looking back over the span of 150 years, one can see that these men and women were suffering from post-traumatic stress disorder. They had survived, but just barely, and the psychological scars would remain forever.

KEEPING THE PEOPLE ALIVE

Amid scenes of increasing desperation, there were food riots in ports in Cork, British troops guarding food shipments were stoned and six landlords were murdered. Responding to growing outrage at home and abroad, the British government decided, as Trevelyan put it, to 'keep the people alive'. While still not providing any direct aid, it passed the *Soup Kitchen Act*, whereby soup kitchens were set up to feed the starving for free, although there were conditions attached.

The demand for soup far exceeded the ability of these groups to provide it. Nevertheless, by the summer of 1847, three million people were kept alive on a half-kilo of 'stirabout' and a 100 gram slice of bread per day. In September, the potato crop appeared — and this time was without blight. But the crop was comparatively tiny, for farmers had been unable to afford seed or were too busy doing public works projects. Consequently, landlords turned to more lucrative sources of income such as wheat or livestock. But, to create the larger fields needed, they had to destroy the dozens of tiny farms and potato plots on their lands — farms to which the starving Irish were desperately clinging.

The solution for the landlords was to evict their Irish tenants and send them out to wander the roads or knock on the doors of the poorhouses. Some paid to send their peasants on ships to North America. These 'coffin ships' were overcrowded and disease-laden. In the summer of 1847, forty ships containing 14,000 Irish waited under quarantine on the St Lawrence River to enter Canada at Quebec. Hundreds died of typhus, their bodies thrown overboard to float past the horrified eyes of the Canadians.

FLIGHT AND REBELLION

Ultimately, during Black '47, about 100,000 Irish crossed the Atlantic to North America. There, they paved the way for a great wave of Irish emigration, consisting of hundreds of thousands

of men and women anxious to find work in a new and bustling country. By the 1870s, Irish immigrants would control the inner political workings of some of America's largest cities, including New York, Boston and Chicago.

Black '47 was the worst year of the famine, but when it was over the Irish continued to suffer. In 1849, after another failed potato crop, things became so bad that young Irishmen got themselves arrested in the hope of being transported to Australia, where at least they would be fed.

Others, tired of British rule and their inhumane response to the famine, proposed drastic political action. A group of rebellious young Irish nationalists plotted to rise against the British. But their leaders were arrested and sentenced to transportation to Australia. However, their passionate writings would influence a future generation of rebels, both in Ireland and America, who would fight to cast off British rule.

As the century wore on, the spectre of famine gradually diminished. Improvements came about such as the diversification of crops and the expansion of railways for transporting food. The working class agitated, with some success, for land reform and achieved along the way a greater awareness of the importance of controlling their own destinies. In this sense, a line can be traced from the Great Hunger to the events that brought about independence from British rule in 1921 and, in 1949, the creation of the Republic of Ireland.

British administrator Sir Charles Trevelyan became notorious for his cruel indifference to human misery.

CUSTER'S LAST STAND

★ ★ ★ ★ ★ ★ ★ ★ ★ ★ ★ ★ ★ ★

The massacre that created an unlikely martyr and spelled the beginning of the end for America's Indian peoples

It took place 130 years ago — on a hot dusty Sunday morning near an obscure river in a remote part of the American West. General George Armstrong Custer and 210 members of the Seventh Cavalry were outnumbered, outflanked and massacred by a massive Sioux army. Certainly, this was General Custer's 'last stand', but it also marked the beginning of the end for the thousands of Sioux warriors who surrounded Custer that day. Public outcry turned Custer into a martyr whose spilled blood had to be avenged, and the American army redoubled its efforts to force the Native American Indians back to the reservations.

★ ★ ★ ★ ★

A colour print of Custer's last fight (painted in 1896) became famous as a Budweiser Brewing Company advertisement.

MOVING WEST

In the late 1860s America continued its westward expansion. It had been slowed by the Civil War between the northern and southern states during 1861–65. The new drive west was fuelled by gold strikes in Colorado and Montana, and white settlers hungry for the rich farmland of the Great Plains.

The tribes that ranged the northern Great Plains were called the Lakota, although the whites, and their Indian foes, would refer to them as the Sioux. The Sioux were a wandering tribe that followed the herds of buffalo and worshipped *Wakan Tanka*, the Great Spirit. By the 1860s, however, the Sioux found a formidable foe swarming into their lands — white men, whom they called *wasichus*, meaning, literally, 'you can't get rid of him'. And so, they underscored their message that white people were not welcome on the land — by slaughtering miners and other incomers, sometimes by broiling them over open fires.

In 1868, the US government and the Sioux signed a treaty. The government would leave much of western South Dakota and eastern Wyoming to the Sioux, and keep settlers and miners away from the Sioux's sacred Black Hills. In return, the Sioux would stop their attacks against whites. By 1876, however, after the discovery of gold in the Black Hills, 15,000 white miners swarmed through Sioux territory. Using Sioux attacks on settlers as an excuse, the administration sent troops to the region with orders to push the Indian tribes further west. This put the Sioux on a collision course with one of the most controversial military figures in American history: George Armstrong Custer.

★ ★ ★ ★ ★

DARING AND DASHING

In June of 1876, Custer's Seventh Cavalry set off as one arm of a three-pronged expedition to find the Sioux, rumoured to have made camp along the Little Bighorn River. One command would move up from the south, another would approach from the west. A third, which included the thirty-one officers and 566 men of Custer's Seventh Cavalry, would approach from the east. When the command approaching from the south was delayed, it was decided to send Custer down the Rosebud River with his regiment. Meanwhile, the other commands travelled along the Bighorn and Little Bighorn Rivers, hoping to trap the Sioux between them.

George Armstrong Custer was reputed to have been the most photographed officer in the Union Army during the Civil War.

George Armstrong Custer was born in 1839, in a small Ohio town, one of five children of a blacksmith father. Custer graduated from West Point military academy in 1861, last in his class. But during the Civil War he quickly earned a reputation as a fierce fighter in the Union Army, which fought against the southern states. He was promoted from first lieutenant to brigadier general (the youngest in the Union Army) — an unheard-of rise in rank.

Not only was Custer brave, but he also had dashing style. He even designed his own uniform made of black velvet, with a brilliant crimson scarf tied round his throat.

Custer's contempt for danger also made him controversial. His cavalry units suffered extraordinarily high casualty rates, even by the bloody standards of the Civil War, because he was known to charge into situations where another commander might proceed more cautiously.

★ ★ ★ ★ ★

ON THE TRAIL OF THE SIOUX

After parting from the army regiments Custer moved his Seventh Cavalry in the direction of the Bighorn Mountains, scouting out Indian trails as they went. All trails seemed to point in the same direction — to the valley of the Little Bighorn River. Custer assumed there was a village there, but he had no idea of its size.

On the morning of 25 June he took his command over the Wolf Mountains and down into the valley of the Little Bighorn, about 25 kilometres from the Indian base. Not completely sure of the location of the village, Custer chose to divide his command into three sections, headed by himself and two other officers. Major Marcus Reno was a nervous, excitable soldier. Captain Frederick Benteen had a reputation as a brave fighter — but he hated Custer with a passion because of what he considered to be Custer's vanity and posturing.

The plan was for Custer to approach the village from the north, and Reno from the south. Benteen, trailing, with pack mules laden with ammunition, would be available to either column, as needed. What Custer did not know was that the Sioux chiefs had decided to band together for protection against the *wasichu* soldiers and had been gathering in the area for months. Now, spread out across a plain on the west bank of the Little Bighorn was a large mass of Indians, an estimated 2000 of whom were warriors. And they knew Custer was coming.

WHERE WAS CUSTER'S SUPPORT?

Did Major Reno and Captain Benteen fail their commander? Almost certainly, yes. Reno's panicked retreat allowed the Indians to corner him, and then concentrate on wiping out Custer. And despite receiving Custer's desperate message begging the captain to come to his aid, Benteen made a decision not to assist, later claiming there were too many hostile Sioux between his position and Custer's. He may have been right. But, never a loyal fan of his commander, he was certainly not likely to go to extraordinary lengths to save him or die in the attempt.

Benteen redeemed himself in some eyes by a courageous performance on Reno Hill, bravely organising the fight against the Sioux with little regard for his own safety. Reno's performance, on the other hand, was said to have had a tinge of hysteria to it — some thought he was drunk — and he was later made the subject of a court of inquiry, although eventually the army dropped all charges against him.

FIRST SKIRMISHES

Reno's men crossed the Little Bighorn River. They were horrified to see, not just one village, but a huge conglomeration of Indian tents extending for 5 kilometres along the banks of the river — six villages in all.

General Custer on horseback, in deadly combat with Native American Indians at the Little Bighorn Battlefield, Montana, in 1876.

At once, a swarm of Indian warriors rose up to meet the advance. Reno led a panicked retreat back across the river and up the banks of a steep bluff. His men finally reached the top and formed a defensive line, where they were joined by Captain Benteen's contingent. Together, their two commands made a stand on the bluff.

Custer's men saw Reno's first skirmish with the Indians and heard the sounds of shots popping. The raw recruits began shouting and cheering. Most of them were poorly trained German or Irish immigrants, fighting not for love of country but for thirteen dollars a month, a bed and three square meals a day.

TOTAL ANNIHILATION

After sending a messenger to tell Benteen to reinforce him, Custer led his force onto a ridge above the village. More and more Indians now flocked in Custer's direction, like 'bees swarming out of a hive', as one Sioux later described it. They fired arcing showers of arrows or made quick, rushing attacks on the cavalry, most of whom had dismounted and shot their own horses to use for cover. A cloud of grey dust and black gunpowder began to obscure the battlefield as the charging Indians gradually divided Custer's forces.

The squads and platoons of the Seventh Cavalry quickly disintegrated under the onslaught. Individuals were then cut down by Indian warriors, who appeared like apparitions out of the smoke and dust. Indian veterans of the battle later told how many of the soldiers did not appear to know how to fight. In their panic, some of these recruits even began shooting each other.

The total annihilation of Custer's force probably took no longer than two hours. One last Indian charge, led by the famous war chief Crazy Horse, swept over the battlefield, and the last survivors went down, shot or speared or clubbed. After that, there was silence and drifting smoke.

At the bluff, Reno's and Benteen's men managed to hold off the Sioux attack for the rest of that day and into Monday afternoon, 26 June. Then, the Sioux, fearing the approach of more soldiers, packed up their tents and moved off to the south in a massive cloud of dust.

★ ★ ★ ★ ★

'THERE HE IS, GOD DAMN HIM'

The next morning, a forward cavalry unit consisting of a lieutenant and Crow Indian scouts rode cautiously through the valley of the Little Bighorn River and saw on a distant hillside numerous objects. At first they thought they were buffalo carcasses and skins drying in the sun. But soon they realised with horror that the objects were the stripped bodies of Custer's entire command, along with their horses.

CUSTER'S BODY WAS DISCOVERED NEAR THE CREST OF A HILL, SURROUNDED BY THE SLAUGHTERED MEMBERS OF HIS STAFF. THE CORPSE WAS RECLINED, SEMI-UPRIGHT AGAINST THE BODIES OF TWO SLAIN SOLDIERS.

At the site, in the hot June sun, the stench was terrible. Sioux squaws, who had swarmed over the battlefield soon after hostilities had ceased, had horribly mutilated the bodies of the slain. A total of 210 men lay dead (a further fifty-three members of Reno's command had died during his desperate fight). Custer's body was discovered near the crest of a hill, surrounded by the slaughtered members of his staff. The corpse was reclined, semi-upright against the bodies of two slain soldiers. He had been shot in the left side near the heart and in the left temple.

Although the public was told afterwards that the Indians had not mutilated Custer's body as a sign of respect for his heroic stature, in fact, after death, his left thigh had been gashed, a finger cut off and an arrow had been driven through his penis. In 1927, a Cheyenne woman told a researcher that the Indian squaws had also punctured Custer's ears with a sewing awl — in order to make him hear better the next time.

But, of course, there would be no next time. An onlooker recalled Captain Benteen rising from Custer's recumbent form and exclaiming, 'There he is, God damn him, he will never fight any more'.

Canadian troops prepare their rifles with bayonets before 'going over the top' on the Western Front in 1916.

THE
WORLD
AT WAR

[1900–1950]

THE BATTLE OF GALLIPOLI

[1915]

★ ★ ★ ★ ★ ★ ★ ★ ★ ★ ★ ★ ★ ★

The catastrophic Allied invasion that helped forge the national identities of three fledgling states

In British history, the allied invasion of the Gallipoli Peninsula in Turkey during World War I is regarded as an embarrassing military debacle. It is remembered chiefly for the fact that it almost cost the young Winston Churchill his career. As a result of the failure of the campaign, he was forced to resign from his job as First Lord of the Admiralty. However, for the peoples of Australia, New Zealand and Turkey, the eight-month-long struggle at Gallipoli emerged as something much more positive and significant. It was the place where their national identities were forged.

In Australia and New Zealand, Gallipoli acquired enormous importance as the place where the courage and spirit of the 'Anzac' fighting man was demonstrated on a world stage for the first time. For the triumphant Turks, defending their ancient Ottoman homeland, Gallipoli was a glorious victory. It would stir up nationalist fervour that would lead to the founding of the Turkish Republic, some eight years later.

Turkish soldiers resting alongside a road, 6 April 1915.

METHOD IN THE MADNESS

There was some sound reasoning behind the original plan for an attack at Gallipoli. By early 1915, the war that had begun only the previous August was at a stalemate, with long lines of trenches running across Western Europe from the North Sea all the way to the Swiss Alps. It was a horrendously violent stalemate: by November 1914, the Allies had suffered nearly a million casualties. British strategists, and in particular Winston Churchill, desperately looked for ways to relieve the pressure on the Western Front.

Soon, they turned their eyes to Asia Minor, and specifically to the Dardanelles Strait, part of the Ottoman Empire. The Ottoman Empire was an ally of the Central Powers (Germany and Austria–Hungary), which were in deadly opposition to England, France and Russia.

The Dardanelles is the narrow neck of water that connects the Aegean Sea to the Black Sea, via the Sea of Marmara and the Bosporus Strait. Today, the city of Istanbul (formerly known as Constantinople) overlooks the Bosporus Strait. In 1914, the British planners saw clearly that if they could gain control of the Dardanelles, and Istanbul, they could gain an important strategic advantage. They would not only neutralise the Ottoman Empire, but also funnel munitions to their ally Russia. This, in turn, could draw German troops away from the deadlocked Western Front.

There were a couple of significant problems facing the Allied forces, however. The narrow strait of the Dardanelles, only 1 to 6 kilometres wide, has a very strong current that makes naval manoeuvres difficult. At the time it was also heavily guarded. The Turks had built forts along the Gallipoli Peninsula, both on the Western European side and the eastern 'Asiatic' side, and had mined the waters of the strait. There was nowhere in the entire 65 kilometre trip up the Dardanelles that a vessel could not be easily reached and sunk by shellfire.

★★★★★

Troops landing at Anzac Cove. The Anzacs successfully penetrated the steep hillsides and scrub-covered ravines that overlooked the beach.

ATTACK BY SEA

In the early winter of 1914–15, the plan was to try to attack the Turkish forts along the Dardanelles using naval power alone. Like most British planners, Churchill considered the Turks to be inferior opponents. In early 1915, a combined fleet of British and French vessels sailed up the Dardanelles to bombard the Turkish defences — only to be pushed back. They suffered heavy losses that included 700 dead, three battleships sunk and three others badly damaged.

Having lost to these 'inferior' Turkish fighters, the British now pulled back to lick their wounds. It was clear they would need the help of an infantry assault. And so the Gallipoli campaign began — as so many other disastrous campaigns have begun — as an escalation after a bitter and humiliating failure.

★ ★ ★ ★ ★

REDIRECTING RESOURCES

Right at the start, there was a dispute over resources. With competing demands for men and supplies from commanders in France, the British high command would allow only half the men requested for the campaign. Also, a significant proportion of the Allied force was to be made up of the green and untried volunteer soldiers of Australia and New Zealand.

The British Twenty-ninth Division was to land at Cape Helles, at the tip of the Gallipoli Peninsula. They would then advance inland and attack the Turkish strongpoints that guarded the Dardanelles. The job of the Anzac troops was to land further north on the west, or Aegean coast, of Gallipoli and move inland to block the expected Turkish retreat from Cape Helles.

★ ★ ★ ★ ★

A RECIPE FOR DISASTER

The Allied landings took place in the pre-dawn darkness of 25 April. The rugged, hilly landscape of much of Gallipoli, with its short, shallow gravel beaches overlooked by heights, was a recipe for disaster. The British took so long to plan their attacks that they lost any advantage, and the 84,000 Turkish troops were able to dig in.

At Helles, the British landing was delayed and it was not until 8 am, in broad daylight, that the British soldiers arrived on shore. They approached on motor launches and on a transport ship, the *River Clyde*, from which 2000 troops disembarked.

The Helles landing was a bloody mess, with the Turks bringing heavy firepower to bear on the invaders from only 50 metres away, blowing the men to bits in their boats. As the soldiers left the *River Clyde* along gangplanks, they provided easy targets for Turkish gunners who shot them down one by one. A British commander flying overhead in a small biplane was horrified to see the clear, bright blue water 'absolutely red with blood' for 50 metres from the beach. Of the first 200 soldiers who disembarked from the *River Clyde*, only twenty-one actually made it to the beach.

At other landing spots along Cape Helles, at beaches designated X, Y and S, the British had more luck, and found

FRATERNISING WITH THE ENEMY

Many soldiers of the British Commonwealth held prejudiced attitudes towards the Turks they would encounter in battle. They were said to be lazy, shiftless cowards, who would run away as soon as fight. These stereotypes gradually evaporated during the months of warfare against the tough and hardened Turkish fighters, who suffered enormous casualties in their defence of Gallipoli. At Anzac Cove, in particular, a mutual respect developed between the adversaries. New Zealand and Australian troops even refused to wear gas masks, asserting that 'the Turks won't use gas. They're clean fighters.' And between the lines, trading went on, with Allied tinned beef and cigarettes being exchanged for sweets and grapes.

themselves landing almost entirely unopposed. By nightfall, 30,000 soldiers were ashore. But at V and W beaches, heavily defended by Turks, the reception was hot. Of 950 Lancashire Fusiliers who landed, five hundred were killed or wounded that morning. A total of two thousand casualties were incurred by the British. In just one day, the slaughter had been horrific and the Allied forces that did get ashore were left clinging desperately to the beachheads.

★★★★★

BIRTHPLACE OF THE ANZAC MYTH

In the dark of the predawn attack, the boats of the Australian and New Zealand troops landed 1500 metres further up the coast at what would soon be immortalised as Anzac Cove. Above the beach towered the Sari Bair range of hills, creased with dead-end gullies and sharp ravines, and covered with thick scrub brush. They were almost impassable. Even so, the Anzac forces made inroads of 1500 metres. However, they were stopped by the quick work of the Turkish commander Mustafa Kemal Ataturk. He ordered a counterattack that drove the Anzacs back, forcing them to dig in on the hillsides, under unremitting fire and blazing sun. Here, too, the Allied forces suffered heavy casualties, with an additional 2000 killed and wounded that day.

★★★★★

STRETCHED TO BREAKING POINT

As the summer months wore on, they brought disease and thirst, endured under the most appalling conditions. Every possible surface was covered by swarms of flies, which had been feeding on the corpses that abounded everywhere. And still the Turks kept coming. After a final Turkish attack failed on 4 May, the Turks dug in again all around the Anzac defences. By then, the Turks had lost 14,000 men, and the Anzacs almost 10,000.

★ ★ ★ ★ ★

THE AUGUST OFFENSIVE

On 6 August, the British made one last-gasp attempt to break the stalemate at Gallipoli with a landing further north, at Suvla Bay. Though two infantry divisions embarked and caught the Turks completely by surprise, the officer in charge failed to exploit this advantage.

At Suvla and at Anzac Cove, up and down each hillside and ridge top, fighting was hand-to-hand and bayonet-to-bayonet. Often the scrub would catch fire, incinerating the attacking Anzac and British troops. But the Turks, inspired by the courageous leadership of Ataturk, continued to hold the high ground along the peninsula. With the stalemate enduring, the Allied campaign was effectively over — except for more bitter slaughter.

★ ★ ★ ★ ★

A SKILFUL RETREAT

Worn down by successive losses, by October, plans were set for an evacuation. In December, the evacuation began, and it turned out that nothing quite became the Allies at Gallipoli like their manner of leaving it. In a departure that salvaged some honour from the debacle, they were able to evacuate 105,000 men right out from under the noses of the Turks. By 9 January 1916 everyone had gone from the shambles of the battlefield.

★ ★ ★ ★ ★

A FOUNDING MYTH

The Gallipoli campaign became an inspiration for the people of Australia and New Zealand, and, in a different way, for the Turks. Known in Turkey as the Battle of Canakkale (after the port in the Dardanelles), Gallipoli was a triumph for the Ottoman Empire. The heroic performance of Ataturk enhanced his military and political influence and saw him become the founder of the modern state of Turkey in 1923.

But it is among Australians and New Zealanders, whose forces had performed so impressively, that the event continues to have its greatest influence. From the horrors of the peninsula, these former colonies, newly separated from their mother country of Great Britain, emerged as fully fledged nations. The pride that Australians and New Zealanders took from Gallipoli and their reverence for their soldiers continue to be manifested as strongly as ever today. The landing is commemorated solemnly in both countries every 25 April, Anzac Day. And, in more recent times, thousands have made pilgrimages, more than ninety years after the event, to the Dardanelles. There they pay their respects on the hallowed ground where their heroes shed so much blood, even if it was for a lost cause.

An official staged image portraying Australian troops charging towards a Turkish trench at Anzac Cove.

THE **BATTLE** OF THE **SOMME**

[1916]

★ ★ ★ ★ ★ ★ ★ ★ ★ ★ ★ ★ ★ ★

Britain's bloodiest day in battle reveals the reality of warfare to a bewildered nation

The 39th Siege Battery provides heavy artillery support at the Battle of the Somme in northern France.

In 1916, from 24 June to 1 July, a total of 3000 British and French guns bombarded the German lines along the Somme River valley in northern France. The massed allied troops were confident that there could be no opposition to such a ferocious onslaught when they went over the top to attack. At 7.20 on the scorching hot morning of 1 July, ten huge mines went off in quick succession right under the German lines — mines that contained hundreds of tonnes of explosives. So certain was the Allied High Command that the Germans had been pulverised that they ordered the British troops to advance. One last rolling barrage of artillery fire would clear their way and conceal their approach. The soldiers' job would be merely to mop up, and then the British cavalry would break through to finish off the retreating Germans.

It took just a few moments for the slaughter to begin, but when it did, it changed British history and British consciousness forever.

★ ★ ★ ★ ★

GRISLY RECORDS

The Battle of the Somme lasted from 1 July to 13 November 1916, and was the most costly battle in the history of the world, with a combined total of 1,265,000 British, French and German dead and wounded. The battle also holds the record for the heaviest loss suffered in one day (1 July) by any British army: 57,450, with 20,000 of these dead.

It was at the Somme that the new British volunteer army was violently blooded. This army consisted for the most part of so-called 'Pals Battalions' — ranks of volunteers recruited from the same rugby clubs, soccer teams and neighbourhoods. The Pals had left their homes to bands playing and flags waving, as if they were marching off not to war but to a big game. The enthusiasm of the Pals Battalions was overwhelming, and matched only by their naivety about war. The first day of the Somme would end all that.

The Somme was by no means the first bloody battle of World War I — the war had, after all, been going on for two years. East of Paris, the terrible Battle of Verdun was still being waged. But the way in which the British fell on the first day, wave after wave of eager Tommies tumbling like ninepins, horrified all who saw it. One German soldier wrote later, there were 'so many we didn't even need to aim'.

★ ★ ★ ★ ★

OVERWHELMING FORCE?

The Somme flows for about 245 kilometres through northern France, from forested highlands and gentle valleys to the English Channel. In 1916, the north of France was a prime battleground, where British forces (north of the Somme) and French forces (south of the river) faced off against the Second German Army. With their superiority in numbers, the French planned to attack the Germans in a battle of attrition, one that would wear the enemy down, forcing them to use up their reserves. However, the massive German attack at Verdun, beginning in February, had tied down most of the French army. It made sense then that the British, under their commander-in-chief Sir Douglas Haig, would take over the planning and provide most of the manpower. The goal now was to launch a major offensive — divert German resources away from Verdun to the Somme, and relieve the pressure on the French.

AS THE ARTILLERY BARRAGE ENTERED ITS FINAL MOMENTS, THE BRITISH WAITED IN THEIR TRENCHES CARRYING THEIR HEAVY PACKS, SMOKING CIGARETTES.

Twenty British divisions would launch an attack on a 24-kilometre front north of the Somme, while seven French divisions charged along a 16-kilometre-wide line 16 kilometres south of the river. Massively powerful (it numbered around 750,000 men), this offensive should have made mincemeat out of the outnumbered sixteen German divisions. But the Allies made the crucial error of depending too much on their artillery. Not only did it destroy any semblance of surprise, but it barely damaged the Germans at all.

STOPPED IN THEIR TRACKS

The first day at the Somme stands as a microcosm of the dreadful cauldron that was World War I. As the artillery barrage entered its final moments, the British waited in their trenches carrying their heavy packs, smoking cigarettes. Officers blew their whistles, and the men then 'stepped off'.

The British battalions attacked in four to seven successive lines, separated by perhaps a hundred or so metres, with the men instructed to walk almost shoulder to shoulder and upright, with their rifles held diagonally across their bodies. Some of the men from the Pals Battalions went into battle that morning with puppies gambolling ahead of them as mascots.

Sergeant Richard Tawney, a thirty-six-year-old writer and teacher in civilian life, jumped off with the first wave of British troops. Initially, things seemed to be going swimmingly, as the unit manoeuvred over four enemy trenches without a hitch. But then 'when we'd topped a little fold in the ground, we walked straight into a zone of machine-gun fire. The whole line dropped like one man.' The sights Tawney saw in that split second haunted him for the rest of his life. Tawney was wounded twice but survived the day. Out of 850 in his company, there were only twenty-four left on the line by 3 July. The Germans were supposed to have been pulverised. What had happened?

★ ★ ★ ★ ★

PERFECT POSITIONING

During the initial advance soldiers like Tawney were astonished to see Germans leaping from their trenches and setting up machine guns in still-smoking shell holes. While the bombardment had been stunning in its ferocity, it had not eroded the Germans' ability to fight. This was mainly because the Germans at the Somme had built not just trenches, but heavy dirt-and-concrete bunkers, some up to 12 metres deep, which no amount of shelling could destroy. Underground passages connected the bunkers (which had amenities such as electricity, and wood-panelling). There were also field hospitals underground, and German reserves waited behind the lines in old caves that the French had used for years to mine chalk.

Adding to this, was the near-perfect German defensive positioning. From their elevated position, the German troops

British troops go over the top of the trenches during a bombardment of artillery fire at the Battle of the Somme.

could easily see what the British were doing; while the British could only observe the Germans' front line.

Not that the offensive was a surprise, of course. The artillery bombardment had given it away, but, even before that, French newspapers had bragged of the coming offensive. And, at 2.45 on the morning of 1 July, German forward listening posts picked up a message from the British commander of the Fourth Army, wishing his soldiers 'Good luck'. It was all the confirmation Berlin needed that the big attack was about to take place.

★ ★ ★ ★ ★

INTO NO-MAN'S-LAND

The German machine guns caught them only a few steps from their trenches, causing bodies to tumble backwards onto those who were climbing up behind. Since thousands and thousands

THE ADVENT OF THE TANK

Tanks were first used in warfare during the Battle of the Somme in an attack by the British Fourth Army on 15 September. The British had fifty of these top-secret weapons, which, unlike modern tanks, were oblong, with huge treads. They could only travel about 3 kilometres an hour, but could easily roll over barbed wire, trenches and machine-gun nests. But shocked German troops soon learned that they were vulnerable to artillery and also to breaking down at crucial moments. While British tanks did achieve some notable successes later in the war, they were not a decisive factor in World War I. Within twenty-five years or so, however, tank warfare would play a crucial part in another war between the same combatants.

of men were moving forwards, the dead and injured were trampled. Still the line kept moving, beyond the British wire, into no-man's-land.

The poet Siegfried Sassoon was in reserve that day (after earning the Military Cross the day before for a daring mission). He sat on a hill behind the lines and watched the British advance through field glasses. 'I am staring at a sunlight picture of Hell', he wrote.

By three o'clock in the afternoon, there was no one moving in no-man's-land except the crawling, moaning wounded, still exposed to machine-gun fire and begging for water as the sun tormented them. Most of the others were dead or had stumbled back into their own trenches.

One fairly typical British division — Eighth Division of III Corps — suffered eighty per cent casualties in the first ten minutes of the advance. It lost 218 out of 300 officers, 5200 out of 8500 soldiers. The German battalions on the opposite side of the wire from Eighth Division lost eight officers and 273 men.

★ ★ ★ ★ ★

A BLOODY STALEMATE

By nightfall of 1 July, the British High Command had realised that the attacks of the first day had failed miserably. Some British officers, including Haig himself, refused to accept the blame for their failed planning — for attacking a well-entrenched enemy in broad daylight after giving ample warning that they were coming! But the ordinary soldier knew what had happened, and most now felt the attack would be called off. Despite the British army having suffered its worst-ever single-day casualty rate, Haig decided to press on.

The British were finally able, on 11 July, to capture the first line of German trenches. But then the Germans brought in reinforcements from Verdun. The contest degenerated into a bloody stalemate, and the slogging war of attrition was drawn

out over a further four months. By November, the British began to make a slow, but steady advance forwards — but then bad weather brought the entire campaign to a halt. By then the casualty figure had reached 1,250,000 for both sides. And the total amount of ground gained since 1 July? Twelve kilometres.

★ ★ ★ ★ ★

DREAMS OF GLORY DASHED

The Germans certainly lost irreplaceable manpower. Yet the battle will forever go down in history as a slaughter that shows what happens when inflexible and unimaginative planning meets rapid-fire automatic weapons.

More than that, the Somme was a turning point in British public opinion about the war. Never again would ordinary people look at the British government, specifically the British High Command, in the same way. After all, it was the Pals Battalions from working-class towns who were decimated at the Somme. Many questioned why these working-class men had been sacrificed in what was evidently a pointless slaughter. Where was the glory of war now? Ever since, the Somme has represented the callousness of upper-class leaders prepared to turn soldiers into cannon fodder.

The transformation of mood, among British troops and among the public at home, was reflected in the diary of a nineteen-year-old British lieutenant named Edwin Campion Vaughan. He had entered the war with dreams of glory and had fought on the front lines for eight months. By the time of the Somme, his attitude had changed completely: 'I sat on the floor and drank whisky after whisky as I gazed into a black and empty future'.

A German soldier mans an observation post at the Somme. He is wearing the distinctive spiked helmet that was later replaced by a sturdier, bowl-shaped helmet.

THE OCTOBER REVOLUTION

[1917]

★ ★ ★ ★ ★ ★ ★ ★ ★ ★ ★ ★ ★ ★ ★

The uprising that created capitalism's strongest rival

On 25 October 1917, American journalist John Reed and his wife, Louise Bryant, were staying at the Hotel Astoria in Petrograd — the former St Petersburg, grand city of the tsars. They woke up that morning to the sounds of bells ringing and trucks racing up and down the street. Leaving their hotel, they learned that the trucks belonged to the Bolsheviks, the revolutionary party headed by Vladimir Ilich Lenin. They carried soldiers who stopped at every street corner to plaster up a proclamation written by Lenin that morning. It read: 'To the Citizens of Russia! The Provisional Government has been deposed. State power has passed into the hands of the organ of the Petrograd Soviet of Workers' and Soldiers' Deputies ... Long live the revolution of workers, soldiers and peasants!'

In fact, the government of the moderate leader Alexander Kerensky had not been deposed at all, but Lenin had decided it wouldn't hurt to stretch the truth a little. And in one important respect, at least, he was right. That morning in Petrograd, the revolution that would change the face of a century — the revolution that 'shook the world', as Reed would write in a famous book on the October Uprising — had truly begun.

A powerful communicator, Vladimir Lenin makes a speech in Red Square on the first anniversary of the Bolshevik Revolution.

The earthquake of the Russian Revolution would create a massive communist empire. Ultimately, it would represent the strongest challenge ever to Western capitalism — a challenge that the West has only recently faced down.

★ ★ ★ ★ ★

Nicholas II was the last Russian tsar. He was deposed during the Russian Revolution and executed by the Bolsheviks in July 1918.

CHANGE LONG OVERDUE

There was little doubt that Russia was in need of a revolution as the twentieth century began. Even though serfdom had been officially abolished in 1861, peasants still worked arduous twelve-hour days six days a week for the small number of wealthy landowners who owned most of the land in Russia. The country had been ruled for centuries by all-powerful tsars of varying abilities, and was mainly governed by a corrupt and crumbling bureaucracy. Common people were treated as little better than animals. Thousands of people existed on the edge of starvation.

Tsar Nicholas II was, even as tsars went, autocratic and conservative. Beginning his reign in 1894, he was unable to see that Russia was changing. The Industrial Revolution had transformed the landscape. Factories had drawn peasants to the cities, in turn bringing them into contact with radical theories and new ways of looking at the world. One of the most appealing was socialism, based on the idea that all men should be equal, that all should have a share of the earth's bounty and no man should have to work for an unjust wage or be a serf.

In 1905, the country underwent a major upheaval. Thousands of Russian workers marched to the Winter Palace in St Petersburg to present a petition to Nicholas, telling him of their grievances. They were unarmed and carried religious banners and pictures of the tsar. In response, the tsar's soldiers opened fire on this peaceful group, killing hundreds. Mass strikes followed, shutting down the country's railways and businesses. Nicholas was forced to issue what was called his October Manifesto, which promised a democratic parliament. But the manifesto was a sham, as the tsar undermined almost any serious effort to allow greater participation in government. Workers and radicals came to realise that yet more drastic action would be required.

★ ★ ★ ★ ★

BOLSHEVIKS AND MENSHEVIKS

The two men who would lead the revolution in 1917, Vladimir Lenin and Leon Trotsky, both spent years in exile as a result of earlier subversive activities. Lenin joined one of the more radical socialist factions and, following fourteen months in jail and exile in Siberia, lectured on the socialist cause throughout Europe.

At a convention of Russian socialist groups that met in 1903 in London (for fear of being targeted in their homeland), Lenin led attempts to create a socialist political party. The delegates split into two groups: the more radical but numerous Bolsheviks and the smaller, more moderate, Mensheviks (of which Trotsky was a prominent member). Both groups played a part in the 1905 uprisings, after which their popularity increased steadily. Soon, all that was needed to fan the flame of revolution was social upheaval — and World War I provided that.

★ ★ ★ ★ ★

DEFEAT SPARKS REBELLION

The massive losses of World War I became the trigger for the Russian Revolution. By the winter of 1917, Russia had lost millions of soldiers — as casualties and prisoners of war, but also to desertion. These deserters, in no mood to knuckle down under the rule of the tsar, returned to their home villages and began seizing land from the wealthy.

In the meantime, food shortages were rampant in the country. In St Petersburg, people were forced to wait in line a total of forty hours a week, just for bread. When they began to riot, this time the troops joined them. With mounting losses from the war, and a complete lack of support from his own government and army, Nicholas II was forced to abdicate in March 1917. The 300-year rule of the Romanov dynasty was at an end, and the tsar and his family were sent into exile in Siberia. A moderate provisional government took over, led by a charismatic, thirty-six-year-old lawyer and politician, Alexander Kerensky.

THE AMERICAN REVOLUTIONARY

John Reed, who famously described the early stages of the Russian Revolution in his 1919 book *Ten Days that Shook the World*, was a controversial figure in his day. He attended Harvard, but then moved to New York and became a socialist, travelling to Mexico in 1913 to witness the Mexican Revolution. With his feminist wife Louise Bryant, he made his way to Russia, where he reported on the revolution. It was very clear from his writings that he was by no means an unbiased observer — in fact, some felt he was used by Lenin and Trotsky as a propaganda tool to get their version of the revolution out to the world at large.

Later, Reed was charged with treason in the United States because he had spoken out against US involvement in World War I. Before his trial, he fled the country and returned to Russia. There is some evidence that he later became disillusioned with the revolution. However, when he died in Russia of typhus in 1920, he became (and still is) the only American to be buried in the Kremlin.

Kerensky was a threat to the more radical groups like the Bolsheviks, whose exiled leaders began making plans to return to Russia. In early April, as Lenin was returning to his homeland, Kerensky was preparing for another Russian offensive against Germany.

When Lenin arrived at Petrograd's Finland Station, he was met by a cheering crowd. He then began planning a revolution that would result in a government run by groups of workers, known as soviets. Leon Trotsky also returned to Petrograd, to agitate on behalf of the Mensheviks.

★ ★ ★ ★ ★

FIGHTING IN THE STREETS

In June, Kerensky launched his offensive against Germany —
with disastrous results. As conditions at the front deteriorated,
rebellious troops commandeered trains and forced the engineers
to drive them to the rear of the lines. Returning to their farms,
they murdered landlords and pillaged the great estates.
Factories in major cities such as Petrograd and Moscow ground
to a halt as workers abandoned their machines and joined the
Bolsheviks. There were food shortages everywhere.

FACTORIES IN MAJOR CITIES SUCH AS PETROGRAD AND MOSCOW GROUND TO A HALT AS WORKERS ABANDONED THEIR MACHINES AND JOINED THE BOLSHEVIKS.

In August Kerensky suffered a disastrous setback. His army
commander-in-chief, General Lavr Kornilov, led an attempted
coup in Petrograd. Kerensky was forced to ask the Bolsheviks
for help. Kornilov was defeated, but not before the Bolsheviks
gained large stores of arms and ammunition. Meanwhile,
Trotsky joined the Bolsheviks. Together, Lenin and Trotsky
created a forceful partnership.

★ ★ ★ ★ ★

THE REVOLUTION BEGINS

On 24 October, Kerensky gave Lenin and Trotsky the opening
they were looking for. In an attempt to nip the Bolshevik
insurrection in the bud, Kerensky cut off the telephone service to
the Bolshevik headquarters, raided the offices of the Bolshevik
newspaper *Pravda*, and sent troops to patrol the streets.

But with little support from his own assembly, Kerensky realised that it would be dangerous to stay in Petrograd any longer. The Bolsheviks had seized key bridges, and his own troops, mainly inexperienced cadets, were deserting. He was almost certain to be captured and executed. Commandeering a car, he fled the city to attempt to find loyal troops to support him.

★ ★ ★ ★ ★

'NO MORE GOVERNMENT'

As John Reed and Louise Bryant walked the streets of Petrograd on 25 October, they found themselves surrounded by excited crowds. There were posters everywhere, addressed, as Reed wrote later, ' … to the peasants, to the soldiers at the front, to the workmen of Petrograd'. Their elation was reflected in the words of one soldier, when questioned by Reed: 'No more government', he answered with a grin. 'Slava Bogu! Glory to God!'

Kerensky's loyal ministers remained in the 1500-room Winter Palace, which was by then surrounded by Bolshevik troops. The siege that followed became one of the strangest in history, almost farcical. The palace was guarded by Kerensky's cadets and old tsarist retainers wearing their royal blue coats. Many of the defenders were drunk.

At about 11 pm, the Bolsheviks fired on the palace using the guns of the Peter and Paul Fortress, an old tsarist fortress built on a small island in the Neva River. Only two shots managed to hit the palace, however, the rest falling harmlessly into the river. They did little more, as Leon Trotsky put it in disgust, than 'injure the plaster'.

Finally, at about 1.30 am, the Bolsheviks broke into the palace and, without bloodshed, arrested the weary cadets and ministers.

★ ★ ★ ★ ★

END GAME

The revolution was never so genteel again. Lenin, now in power, named as ministers the likes of Leon Trotsky and Joseph Stalin. Lenin had the tsar and his family murdered, as well as other prominent Romanovs. A civil war spread across the nation, a vicious, take-no-prisoners battle between the newly formed Red Army and the 'Whites', a coalition of tsarist supporters and other conservatives backed by the governments of Great Britain, France and the United States. These nations were extraordinarily worried about the threat that a communist Russia might pose to their democracies and their economic interests.

By 1920, the Bolsheviks, now officially renamed the Russian Communist Party, had triumphed. Kerensky fled to Paris and made his way to the United States, where he died in 1970. After Lenin's death from a stroke in 1924, there was a bitter power struggle. His obvious successor, Trotsky, was ousted and forced to flee by Joseph Stalin, who later had Trotsky assassinated in Mexico City.

Stalin became the premier of the Soviet state for the next twenty years, and was responsible for the deaths of millions of the very people the revolution was supposed to free from oppression. Russia had been liberated from the cruel and inept rule of the tsars. But the unfortunate result was the replacement of the tsars with an equally cruel and inefficient state.

On 25 October 1917, armed with rifles, the revolutionaries systematically occupied key parts of the city.

D-DAY

[1944]

★ ★ ★ ★ ★ ★ ★ ★ ★ ★ ★ ★ ★ ★

The daring invasion that was the beginning of the end for Hitler

At about 2.30 on the cloudy morning of 6 June 1944, three divisions of Allied paratroopers — about 20,000 men — took off from airfields in southern England and flew east. The planes kept formation until they hit the French coast, when heavy anti-aircraft fire and machine guns reached up for them. Bullets passed through the thin skins of the lumbering C-47 transport aircraft, sounding, one man remembered, like 'corn popping'.

Some planes were hit and exploded in mid-air. Others crashed into the ground below, burning. Still others took evasive action, scattering across the night skies. Levelling off where they could, the pilots gave the signal and the jumpmasters ordered the paratroopers out the door. The US paratroopers' goal was to block off approaches to the Normandy beaches; the British strategy was to seize bridges over the Orne River.

Meanwhile, at dawn, from the vantage point of what would become known as Utah Beach, German gunners looked out to sea as the mist began to lift slowly from the water. Blinking in disbelief, they saw before them the greatest amphibious landing force in the history of the world — 6500 ships spread out in the English Channel along an 80 kilometre stretch of Normandy's coast. In those ships, and others still in port in England, a total of 150,000 soldiers waited to land. Overhead, were B-17s, each

Allied soldiers disembark a military ship off the Normandy coastline as part of Operation Overlord.

carrying sixteen 225 kilogram bombs with which to pulverise the German coastal defences — just part of the force of 11,500 aircraft that would attack that day.

★ ★ ★ ★ ★

OPERATION OVERLORD

The Germans were witnessing the beginning of Operation Overlord, the long-awaited Allied invasion of France. Both sides had known for some time that the only way the Allies could destroy the German defences in Europe would be with a major land offensive. With progress slow on other fronts in Europe, only a major ground offensive from the west was going to break the stalemate. And using Britain as a staging area for the hundreds of thousands of troops needed was the only possible approach.

The question for the Germans was: where along the Channel coast would the Allies attack? The Germans' Atlantic defences extended all the way from Scandinavia to Spain, but they could not possibly station enough troops to repel an invasion at every point. So the Germans had placed their bets on Pas de Calais, the region around the port of Calais. This was the area of France closest to England and could provide deep-water harbours for Allied ships, as well as a direct route to Paris.

To take advantage of these German assumptions, Allied planners launched a massive disinformation campaign, code-named Operation Fortitude. It involved fake radio traffic, dummy troop emplacements, even German 'spies' in England who were really Allied agents — all to make the Germans believe that an attack on the Pas de Calais was imminent.

Meanwhile, the Allies developed a plan for a massive offensive on the Normandy coast, Operation Overlord. The commander of the operation was US General Dwight D. Eisenhower. General Bernard Montgomery of the British army led the Allied ground forces. Preparations were meticulous and

Allied Expeditionary Force Supreme Commander Eisenhower (left) and senior British commander Field Marshall Montgomery (right) confer on invasion plans.

extended over a period of two years with a steady build-up of troops and equipment. At the time of the invasion, the total number of combat-ready troops was 800,000.

Five beaches would be assaulted by Allied divisions: moving from east to west, they were code-named Sword (to be targeted by the British Third), Juno (Canadian Third), Gold (British Fiftieth), Omaha (US First and Twenty-ninth) and Utah (US Fourth).

★ ★ ★ ★ ★

'THE MOMENT OF OUR LIFE'

After the Allied bombers had pounded the German shore defences, the navy began a massive bombardment in an attempt to destroy the gun emplacements, as well as mines and other obstacles at the water's edge. One newspaper correspondent described the bombardment as 'the loudest thing I have ever heard in my life'.

At 6.20 in the morning, the bombardment let up and US landing craft approached Omaha Beach, which was now shrouded in smoke. Shortly after, the invasions began at Juno, Sword, Gold and Utah. Unfortunately, the bombardment had done little to destroy the German defences. This was a testament to the work of Field Marshal Erwin Rommel, commander of the German Seventh and Fifteenth Armies, who had insisted that the German pillboxes be made of thick concrete reinforced with steel rods.

On Juno Beach, Canadian casualties in the first wave were fifty per cent overall. But those who made it ashore, backed up by the dependable amphibious tanks, were able to help neutralise the pillboxes. By afternoon, they were off the beach and fighting house-to-house in the village of Courseulles-sur-Mer.

But less than a kilometre away, the western edge of the beach was severely battered by machine-gun fire from the pillboxes. There, the Canadian artillery bombardment had completely missed the mark and the tanks meant to support the men had landed elsewhere by mistake. The subsequent slaughter was terrifying. Though they finally made it past the beach defences, three-quarters of their company were lost. By the end of the day, however, the Canadian Third Infantry had pushed further into France than any other unit.

★ ★ ★ ★ ★

HELP FROM HOBART'S FUNNIES

On Sword Beach, the British were confronted with minefields and beach obstacles, but fortunately they came equipped with one of the oddest-looking weapons of the war: tanks known as Hobart's Funnies. (They were named after their inventor, Percy Hobart.) Some of these vehicles had been modified to carry long arms like giant rolling pins, which whipped heavy chains into the sand, exploding mines harmlessly. Others carried long extending platforms that could span ditches and walls.

THE SUBSEQUENT SLAUGHTER WAS TERRIFYING. THOUGH THEY FINALLY MADE IT PAST THE BEACH DEFENCES, THREE-QUARTERS OF THEIR COMPANY WERE LOST.

The British eventually managed to land 28,000 troops (suffering only 600 casualties) and push to within 6 kilometres of their target, the key town of Caen, before German counterattacks stalled them.

On Gold Beach, the British suffered heavy casualties initially, in part because their tanks went astray. But by the end of the day, they, too, were advancing off the beach.

American paratroopers drop into Normandy behind enemy lines, on or near D-Day. Their rescue would depend on a successful Allied sea assault.

A MOVING TARGET

One of the most daring assaults on that day was the attack by the US Second Rangers on Pointe du Hoc, a 30-metre-high promontory of land that juts up between Omaha and Utah beaches. Here, the Germans had emplaced six 155 millimetre artillery guns that could wreak havoc on troops on both Utah and Omaha. The Rangers had trained intensively to capture these guns by scaling the cliffs using ropes and metal extension ladders that had been provided by a London fire company. Under heavy fire, they reached the top of the cliffs — only to discover that the guns had been moved about 1500 metres inland and replaced with dummy wooden guns under camouflage netting. Undeterred, the Rangers found the guns and destroyed them, and then held off repeated German counterattacks.

At Utah Beach, despite earlier mass confusion, the German defences were quickly silenced, the seawall breached, and men and equipment began to pour ashore.

★ ★ ★ ★ ★

OMAHA'S DAUNTING DEFENCES

Historians have commented that if there was one place where the Germans might have stopped the Allied onslaught in Normandy, it was at Omaha Beach. Because it was the only stretch of open beach for some way, it was considered an obvious target for landing, and the Germans made sure it was heavily defended. Yet the Allies had no choice but to attack at Omaha — if they picked a beach further west, there would be too great a gap between them and the British sectors.

Omaha Beach is about 10 kilometres long and perhaps 400 metres across at low tide, which is when the invasion was occurring. Much of the ground was shingle, which would not support the weight of tanks. With high bluffs facing the beach and on either side of it, the Americans could not outflank the German defences. They had to go right at them.

And what defences they were. Every centimetre of ground along the beach was pre-sighted by machine guns, mortars and artillery. Five 'draws' (or small ravines) led up the cliffs; and overlooking each was a strongpoint containing the dreaded German 88, a light artillery gun.

When the German defenders saw the Americans swarming ashore that morning, they almost felt sorry for them. 'They must be crazy', one of them said. 'Are they going to swim ashore? Right under our muzzles?'

★ ★ ★ ★ ★

WITHERING FIRE

But right under their muzzles the Americans came — 40,000 of them over the course of the day. With heavier than expected tidal currents caused by strong winds, by the time they landed, the soldiers had been in their boats for four hours. They were wet, seasick and exhausted. When the first landing craft hit the beach, it was literally pulverised, either by a mine or German artillery fire, killing all the soldiers on board. Other GIs (a generic term for an American soldier) hit the beach at the same time, but withered under the volume of fire (one German machine-gunner alone fired 12,000 rounds that day). Many of the landing craft were stopped by the barrage and let their ramps down too early, causing the heavily loaded troops to disembark into deep water. A good many soldiers drowned.

Men ran onto the beach and then froze in fear. One survivor remembered: 'The beach was covered with bodies, men with no legs, arms — God it was awful'. Bad as the firepower was, if the attackers simply stayed where they were, they would die. They had to move, and, one by one, groups of men raced for the seawall near the base of the cliff. Though the machine-gun fire from above could not reach them they were still subject to murderous mortar fire. As waves of men followed, the GIs were able to force their way up the draws and, once on top of the cliffs, attack the German fortifications from the rear.

THOUGH THE MACHINE-GUN FIRE FROM ABOVE COULD NOT REACH THEM THEY WERE STILL SUBJECT TO MURDEROUS MORTAR FIRE. AS WAVES OF MEN FOLLOWED, THE GIS WERE ABLE TO FORCE THEIR WAY UP THE DRAWS AND, ONCE ON TOP OF THE CLIFFS, ATTACK THE GERMAN FORTIFICATIONS FROM THE REAR.

There were more than 3000 casualties on Omaha Beach that day, and most occurred in the first few hours. By nightfall, however, the Americans had a precarious toehold.

★ ★ ★ ★ ★

A FATAL DELAY

Allied forces suffered 11,000 casualties on D-Day, but managed the most important thing in any amphibious assault: not to be driven back into the sea. Over the next week or so, the troops were able to form a secure area 130 kilometres long and 16 kilometres deep. The German commanders, many of whom thought the real invasion was still to come at Pas de Calais, were slow to react, and by the time it finally dawned on them that Normandy was the Big One, the Allies were too securely settled in to drive out.

In late July, the British and Canadians mounted major offensives. These drew more and more German reserves, allowing the Americans, further to the west, to break out from the coast. Allied forces then pushed through France en masse and by August had captured Paris. The success of the D-Day landing meant that Hitler's Third Reich was all but doomed.

THE BOMBING OF HIROSHIMA

[1945]

★ ★ ★ ★ ★ ★ ★ ★ ★ ★ ★ ★ ★ ★ ★

How the most powerful weapon yet created ended World War II, began the Cold War and raised the spectre of nuclear catastrophe

★ ★ ★ ★ ★

On 6 August 1945, the United States dropped an atomic bomb on the Japanese city of Hiroshima — and changed the world utterly. Three days later, another was unleashed on Nagasaki. In the short run, these massive weapons of destruction ended World War II almost immediately. In the long run, the unleashing of atomic weapons would give rise to the Cold War during which the great superpowers, the United States and the Soviet Union, engaged in a nuclear arms race.

The mushroom cloud from 'Little Boy', the first atomic bomb (dropped on 6 August 1945), rises above the city of Hiroshima.

RELATIVELY UNSCATHED

With a population of some 250,000 people, Hiroshima still had the feel of a small, peaceful town. Located in the western part of Japan's main island of Honshu, mountains flanked the city on three sides and seven rivers flowed through it. More than forty bridges crossed these rivers, the largest and most famous one being the Aioi Bridge.

Why hadn't the Americans bombed them, the people of Hiroshima often asked themselves? As July turned into early August, Hiroshima's luck continued. When the town's children saw the silver shapes of the US B-29 bombers high in the sky, winging their way elsewhere in the country, they would laugh and cry out, 'B-san!' Which means, 'Mr B'.

★ ★ ★ ★ ★

A RUTHLESS CAMPAIGN

After their initial successes in China and South-east Asia, the Japanese had been slowly pushed back towards their homeland. By June, 1944, the Americans arrived within striking distance of Japan and were able to unleash the might of their air force. The mainstay of that force was the four-engine B-29 Superfortress, with its cutting-edge innovations.

THE PURPOSE OF THIS BOMBING CAMPAIGN, AIMED DIRECTLY AT JAPAN'S CIVILIAN POPULATION, WAS TO FORCE THE COUNTRY TO SURRENDER.

At first, however, the bombing results that came from Japan were disappointing. But then General Curtis E. LeMay was appointed to take over the bombing campaign. An inspirational figure in the US military during World War II, LeMay conceived the tactic of low-level, night-time bombing raids using incendiaries.

LeMay's perfect storm of tactics came together on the night of 9–10 March 1945 with the bombing of Tokyo. A total of 335 B-29s went in low and slow, dropping incendiaries or napalm every 15 metres. Within two hours, Tokyo was engulfed in a firestorm. Estimates of the dead civilians that night range from 70,000 to a 100,000. One million Japanese were left homeless.

During the raid, American pilots were forced to wear oxygen masks to filter out the stench of burning flesh. The purpose of this bombing campaign, aimed directly at Japan's civilian population, was to force the country to surrender. However, the ferocious fighting on the Japanese islands of Iwo Jima and Okinawa that spring had made the American High Command realise that Japan would not give in easily. Even more extraordinary force was needed.

★ ★ ★ ★ ★

'THE PERFECT AIMING POINT'

On the morning of 6 August, nurses in Shima Hospital, next to Hiroshima's Aioi Bridge, woke their patients for breakfast while children and their teachers gathered at the Honkawa Elementary School next door. Around 7.30, an American B-29 flew overhead and seemed to circle, but the children in the Honkawa school playground paid 'Mr B' little heed.

Just after eight o'clock, another US bomber appeared. This one, too, was ignored by the nurses, teachers and children, and by the citizens of Hiroshima who hurried across the Aioi Bridge to work. At the same moment, high above Hiroshima, a twenty-six-year-old American bombardier named Major Thomas Ferebee, aboard the second B-29 (the first had been a weather-monitoring plane), squinted through his bombsight, searching for that very same bridge. Ferebee had personally selected the Aioi Bridge from reconnaissance photographs as his Aiming Point, or AP. His commander, Colonel Paul Tibbets, the pilot of the B-29, had agreed with his choice, saying, 'It's the most perfect AP I've seen in the whole damned war'.

It was just after 8.15 am. The 'perfect AP' filled Ferebee's precision bombsight and he said: 'I've got it'.

★ ★ ★ ★ ★

A DEADLY DILEMMA

The 4.5 tonne bomb Ferebee was about to release was called 'Little Boy', and it was the first of only two atomic bombs in history to be used in conflict. Little Boy was the end result of the most extraordinary secret program of the war.

After nuclear fission had shown that enormous energy could be released by splitting an atom, Germany had begun developing an atomic bomb. In response, the Americans, Canadians and British had initiated the Manhattan Project in 1942 to develop one, too. Costing over two billion US dollars, the program eventually produced a nuclear weapon. The 'gadget', as the scientists called it, was successfully detonated in New Mexico on 16 July 1945.

The new weapon gave US President Harry S. Truman a chance to end the war quickly. But whether dropping such a bomb on Japanese civilians was morally acceptable was an immensely problematic issue. Truman was also under intense pressure to limit the further loss of life that would result from a drawn-out conflict with the Japanese. The war in Europe and the Pacific had cost almost 300,000 American lives, and the death toll was soaring in the continuing war with Japan. If the Americans went ahead with their planned invasion of the Japanese mainland by conventional means, they could expect casualties in the hundreds of thousands, as well as millions of Japanese deaths.

On 26 July, America joined with its Allies, demanding Japan's unconditional surrender. Japan refused and seemed to dismiss the Allied demands out of hand. (In fact, Japan was in turmoil. Its leaders were terrified that the Soviet Union might enter the war against it — which it did, on 8 August.)

Even at this point, Truman still had alternatives to dropping the atomic bomb immediately, including demonstrating its power

The street of Kawara-machi in the peaceful city of Hiroshima, before the destruction of the atomic bomb.

on a non-civilian target. But, tiring of the Japanese delays, he decided to proceed with the most forceful demonstration possible.

After some discussion, the peaceful city of Hiroshima was picked as the target. Because it had not yet been bombed, the destruction caused by Little Boy could be better studied. Also, the mountains on three sides of the city would have a 'focus effect' on the blast, causing more casualties.

★ ★ ★ ★ ★

SHOCKING DESTRUCTION

As soon as Little Boy was released, the B-29 — called the *Enola Gay*, after Paul Tibbets' mother — headed back west, towards the sea. Ferebee watched the bomb as it fell, at first sideways, then turning nose down. It was set to detonate in forty-three seconds and the crew waited breathlessly.

Nothing happened after the forty-three-second count, and many of the crew thought the bomb was a dud. But then there came an extraordinary flash of light followed by a fierce shock wave. A huge column of smoke began to rise from a fiery red core, forming a mushroom-shaped cloud. Co-pilot Captain Robert Lewis wrote in his notes as the plane sped from the target: 'My God, what have we done?'

★ ★ ★ ★ ★

GROUND ZERO

Ferebee missed the Aioi Bridge by about 250 metres, and Little Boy exploded at 560 metres above Shima Hospital. The hospital courtyard was directly under the explosion and was thus the Ground Zero, or 'hypocentre', of the blast. All hospital staff and patients were instantly vaporised. Eighty-eight per cent of people within 500 metres died instantly. Heat waves at temperatures of 3000 degrees Celsius caused first-degree burns within about 3 kilometres of Shima Hospital.

The Aioi Bridge buckled but was not destroyed. At the Honkawa Elementary School about 100 metres away, teacher Katsuko Horibe was tossed through the air but survived, as did the only other survivors near the blast, because the school had concrete walls. The children in the playground were burned beyond recognition.

The Ota River, spanned by the Aioi Bridge, was the first place people raced to, to dive into the water, but the river was filled with burning debris and burning bodies. Scenes of horror abounded. A black rain began to fall an hour after the attack, yet it did not put out any of the fires.

SHOW OF STRENGTH?

Some historians, particularly in the 1960s, believed that the Truman Administration was mainly motivated by fear of the Russians. The atomic bomb would be a display of U.S. power to the communist government of Joseph Stalin. Russia at the time was considering entering the war against Japan; the Truman administration saw such a move as a bald-faced power grab. Dropping the bomb, some say, was a way to cause the Russian bear to back off — and to keep it from sharing in the spoils of a defeated Japan. In fact, the US Secretary of State, James Byrnes, did tell Truman that the bomb should be dropped so that 'Moscow would not [get in] on the kill'. And whether or not this became Truman's main motivation, the dropping of the bomb may well have kept the Soviets from demanding a joint occupation of Japan, which Stalin had been hinting at only a week prior to the attack on Hiroshima.

A view of the bomb-damaged Hiroshima Prefecture Industrial Promotion Hall. It is now known as the A-bomb Dome, part of the Hiroshima Peace Memorial Park.

One witness to the horror, a fifteen-year-old girl who was disfigured by the blast, remembered: 'I saw something shining in the clear blue sky. I wondered what it was, so I stared at it. As the light grew bigger, the shining thing got bigger as well ... there was a flash, far brighter than one used for a camera.

It exploded right in front of my eyes … The dust was rising and something sandy and slimy entered my mouth.' It was her blood mixed with the dust.

★ ★ ★ ★ ★

'THE GREATEST DAY IN HISTORY'

Estimates of the death toll vary, but perhaps one hundred thousand people died in Hiroshima almost immediately, and another 30,000, due to burns and radiation poisoning, by the end of the year. President Truman declared 6 August 'the greatest day in history', and again called on Japan to surrender, promising 'a rain of ruin from the air' if it again refused.

But the shocked Japanese government did not respond immediately and on 9 August another atomic bomb was dropped, this time on Nagasaki, where the death toll reached 60,000 to 70,000. After this, on 15 August, Japan surrendered.

The war was over. But the horror at the use of the nuclear bomb echoed through subsequent generations. After 6 August 1945, human beings would always be possessed of the knowledge that there exists a weapon that can do awful damage, and can be carried in a missile-tip or even a suitcase. Not only that, but the use of just one of these weapons might cause yet more of them to be unleashed — and the world might ultimately be destroyed. This consciousness, called nuclear anxiety, is a fixture of our modern age, and is here to stay.

This German man expresses the elation shared by many Germans at the fall of the Berlin Wall.

THE
COLD WAR
AND BEYOND
[1950–2001]

THE ASSASSINATION OF PRESIDENT KENNEDY

[1963]

★ ★ ★ ★ ★ ★ ★ ★ ★ ★ ★ ★ ★ ★

The slaying of a much-loved leader leaves a nation in shock and gives birth to countless conspiracy theories

President Kennedy, First Lady Jacqueline Kennedy and Texas Governor John Connally ride through the streets of Dallas, 22 November 1963.

Almost everyone in the Western world who was old enough at the time can remember where they were and what they were doing on 22 November 1963, when they heard the news that President Kennedy had been assassinated in Dallas, Texas. The young, charismatic American president had won international renown as the gracious, charming symbol of a World War II generation's coming of age, of the beginning of a 'New Frontier' that would include the end of the Cold War, the end of poverty and the spread of democracy across the globe. The shock of his death reverberated far and wide.

Without doubt, the assassination is the single-most controversial event in U.S. history. Well over 2000 books have been written on the subject. Two government commissions have studied it in depth. Numerous movies and documentaries have been devoted to dissecting that day, those scant six seconds, those three (or four, or five) shots.

★ ★ ★ ★ ★

GOING ON A CHARM OFFENSIVE

The day of the assassination began for the glamorous presidential couple in Fort Worth, Texas, about 50 kilometres from Dallas. Texas was one of the states in the country not swayed by the Kennedy aura. In particular, Kennedy's stance on civil rights did not endear him to the hearts of conservative Texans. Because numerous violent fringe groups were known to exist in Dallas, security along the president's motorcade route would be stringent.

★ ★ ★ ★ ★

A VIOLENT LONER

As Kennedy was preparing to leave Fort Worth, a twenty-four-year-old man named Lee Harvey Oswald was preparing to leave for his job at the Texas School Book Depository. The textbook distribution centre was located in Dealey Plaza, on the outskirts of Dallas's downtown. Oswald had a bland, almost meek appearance that disguised numerous secrets. Born into a poor New Orleans family, he had never known his father, who had died two months before his birth. He grew up to be a lonely child — 'lone' or 'loner' were words that would follow him all his short life — who was fascinated with guns. As a teenager, he developed leftist views. He could also be violent, striking his mother, Marguerite, on several occasions; once he pulled a knife on her.

Photographed in his backyard, Lee Harvey Oswald holds a Mannlicher-Carcano rifle and Marxist newspapers. Some have questioned the authenticity of this photo.

Despite his early socialist leanings, Oswald joined the US Marines when he was seventeen, in 1956. After only a few weeks of training, he had attained a 'sharpshooter' qualification on the firing range. That meant he could hit a 25 centimetre bull's-eye from 200 metres away, eight times out of ten, without the aid of telescopic sight.

★ ★ ★ ★ ★

THE FATEFUL JOURNEY

President Kennedy and his entourage — which included Vice President Lyndon Johnson, a native Texan, and his wife, Lady Bird, as well as Texas Governor John Connally and his wife, Nellie — flew into Dallas's Love Field to be greeted by cheering crowds. There was special applause for a smiling Jackie Kennedy, lovely in a pink suit and pillbox hat. The Kennedys and Connallys then entered their limousine (the Johnsons would follow two cars behind) for the motorcade to the Dallas Trade Mart, where Kennedy would make a speech. The Kennedy car was an open-topped Lincoln Continental.

LEE HARVEY OSWALD, ALONE ON THE SIXTH FLOOR IN THE SOUTH-EAST CORNER OF THE BUILDING, HAD A BIRD'S-EYE VIEW OF PROCEEDINGS.

The motorcade would pass through Dealey Plaza, in front of the Texas School Book Depository building. Lee Harvey Oswald, alone on the sixth floor in the south-east corner of the building, had a bird's-eye view of proceedings. In his hands was an Italian-made Mannlicher-Carcano rifle, complete with telescopic scope, which he had purchased for $24.45 from a Chicago mail-order company. Conspiracy theorists would later disparage the rifle, but FBI tests found it to be extremely accurate. It fired a 6.5 mm bullet at about 600 metres a second. It could also be broken down and reassembled quickly. (Oswald had walked into work that day with a long brown package that contained, he said, 'curtain rods'.)

By noon, Oswald was ready.

★ ★ ★ ★ ★

THE MAN BEHIND THE BOXES

A study of Lee Harvey Oswald reveals a personality typical of lone assassins. After a short, unhappy time in the Marine Corps, his Marxist leanings became more pronounced. He moved to the Soviet Union, where he worked in a factory in Minsk and met and eventually married Marina Nikolayevna Prusakova. But after an attempt to obtain Soviet citizenship failed, he tried to kill himself and was placed in a mental asylum.

Upon his release, Oswald returned to America and settled in the Dallas–Fort Worth area with Marina and their new daughter, June. When he wasn't working in a series of menial jobs, Oswald made fitful attempts to live out his socialist beliefs. He volunteered briefly in Cuba, and went to Mexico, where he visited both the Cuban and Soviet embassies, trying to get visas to live in their countries.

All of this later provided fodder for conspiracy theorists, who believed that Oswald was working for the Russians or the Cubans, or even the CIA. A problem with all these theories, however, is Oswald's extraordinary instability. He was just too weird for professional intelligence operatives to use as a spy, let alone as an assassin.

★ ★ ★ ★ ★

THE ZAPRUDER TAPE

Even today, voicing the theory that Oswald was the 'lone' shooter can prompt a vitriolic response from passionate conspiracy theorists. 'Ridiculous!' they say, or 'What about Umbrella Man?' Umbrella Man is a figure who appears in a famous film of the assassination. For no apparent reason, on a sunny day, he opens and closes his umbrella just as Kennedy's motorcade passes and shots ring out. Many conspiracy theorists suggest that this man must have been signalling to someone.

The film in question was made by Abraham Zapruder, a fifty-eight-year-old clothing manufacturer and great supporter

One of the photographs presented to the Warren Commission showing the presidential motorcade on the day of the assassination.

of President Kennedy. To record the president's visit, he chose a vantage point on a concrete pergola near the triple underpass through which Kennedy's motorcade would drive. The innocent and enthusiastic film Zapruder subsequently made has become essential evidence in all investigations of the assassination.

★ ★ ★ ★ ★

KENNEDY'S LAST MOMENTS

Just before 12.30 pm, Kennedy's motorcade turned left onto Elm Street beneath the book depository. The 120-degree turn slowed the motorcade down to a speed of just 16 kilometres per hour.

CONGRESSIONAL FINDINGS DISCREDITED

In 1976, the US House of Representatives convened a congressional committee to hear new evidence on both the Kennedy assassination and the later assassination of Martin Luther King. Their 1979 conclusion regarding Kennedy was that, while Oswald had fired three shots and killed the president, acoustical evidence presented a 'high probability' that two more shots were fired at Kennedy from somewhere on Dealey Plaza, indicating the presence of a conspiracy.

The committee was relying on evidence that has now been discredited, however, particularly a Dictabelt recording from the motorcycle of a Dallas police officer, which supposedly picked up the sound of other shots. The police officer insisted that he was not in Dealey Plaza at the time the 'shots' were recorded, but racing with the Kennedy limousine to the hospital. In 1982, a team of scientists backed him up, concluding that the sound of 'shots' on the tape is probably static.

First came two motorcycles, then Kennedy's limousine, with the President and First Lady in the back seat and John and Nellie Connally in the front seat. The crowds along Elm Street began to scream and wave. 'Mr President', Nellie Connally said at that moment, 'you can't say that Dallas doesn't love you!' It was at this point, as Kennedy and his wife smiled and waved, that Oswald fired his first shot. It missed.

Within three seconds, Oswald had fired again. This second shot entered Kennedy's upper back. The same bullet then struck John Connally, seriously injuring him.

Watching the Zapruder film at this point, one sees the situation in the lead limousine quickly unravel into chaos. The driver, disastrously, slows the vehicle to a near crawl. Governor Connally has collapsed with his head on his wife's lap. Kennedy is leaning towards Jackie. As she reaches to him, suddenly, a large portion of the right side of Kennedy's skull flies off. The bullet had entered the back of Kennedy's head and exploded outwards. Nellie Connally remembers Jackie Kennedy saying, 'His brains are in my hand.'

The film captures Jackie, her pink suit blood-spattered, trying to climb over the back of the car, where a Secret Service man was reaching to her. Some speculated that she was trying to escape the carnage, but she later provided a simple explanation: a piece of her husband's skull had blown back over the car. She wanted to get it, in case it was needed.

★ ★ ★ ★ ★

'JUST A PATSY'

After hiding the rifle at the book depository, Oswald returned to his boarding house, picked up a pistol and headed out once more. His behaviour — ducking into storefronts as police cars went by — soon attracted attention and an officer named J.D. Tippit stopped him for questioning. Oswald shot him four times and killed him.

By this time, the rifle had been found and an all-points bulletin had been issued for Oswald's arrest. Soon, he was caught in a movie theatre where he was hiding and booked on suspicion of murdering both President Kennedy and Officer Tippet. He claimed to reporters who visited him briefly that he was innocent, 'just a patsy', arrested because he had lived in the Soviet Union.

ALTHOUGH HE CONTINUED TO DENY KILLING THE PRESIDENT, HE SEEMED TO BE ENJOYING HIMSELF IMMENSELY – RIGHT UP TO THE MOMENT WHEN, WHILE BEING TRANSFERRED TO ANOTHER JAIL, HE WAS SHOT AND KILLED BY A STRIP CLUB OWNER NAMED JACK RUBY.

Meanwhile, the enormity of the assassination was sinking in. Film taken of the crowd after the motorcade rushed the mortally wounded president to the hospital shows men and women standing around in stunned silence. The same reaction of shock, disbelief and grief quickly spread worldwide.

★★★★★

OSWALD IS SILENCED

In his short time in custody, Oswald continuously wore a smug grin or sneer. Although he continued to deny killing the president, he seemed to be enjoying himself immensely — right up to the moment when, while being transferred to another jail, he was shot and killed by a strip club owner named Jack Ruby.

Ruby's motive appeared to be simple revenge: he had idolised Kennedy. Conspiracy theorists claimed Ruby had been hired by the 'Mob' to shut Oswald up. But Ruby's Mafia connections were never proven. Ruby was convicted of murdering Oswald in 1964 but died in jail of lung cancer in 1966, insisting on his deathbed that 'there was no one else' involved in Oswald's murder.

Despite this, and findings of the 1966 Warren Commission, which stated that Oswald had been the lone gunman, theorists continued to pore over pictures of Dealey Plaza on that day, looking for accomplices. They found smoke coming from the grassy knoll, which turned out to be leaf shadows. They found CIA men disguised as tramps, who turned out to be tramps. Shots that seemed to have come from all over the plaza turned out to be acoustical echoes.

Oh, and Umbrella Man? The simple truth about Umbrella Man is that he was a guy named Louie Witt, who came forward in 1978 when he heard of his notoriety among conspiracy theorists. Witt was an eccentric who waved his umbrella to heckle Kennedy; he still had the umbrella.

And the simple truth about the assassination appears to be that Lee Harvey Oswald, acting on a deranged impulse, was the sole killer of John F. Kennedy. Not a terribly satisfying answer — as mundane, in fact, as an old umbrella — but, nonetheless, unless new evidence is found, almost certainly the correct one.

THE FIRST MOON LANDING

[1969]

America's rapid triumph in the space race brings lunar exploration to a halt

It's always been up there, 383,000 kilometres away, beautiful and remote, waxing and waning, in charge of tidal pulls. Human beings have worshipped it, steered by it and been driven mad by it. But no one had ever set foot on it.

It took two things to make a lunar expedition possible in the late 1960s. First, technology had to advance to a point where rocketry could hurl capsules out of the Earth's gravitational field. Second, the Russians had to appear to be getting there first. At the height of the Cold War, landing a man on the Moon was, first and foremost, a political act. The United States and Russia were competing in every aspect of life, from education and technology to the arms race. Landing a man on the Moon would demonstrate the superiority of one system — democracy or communism over the other.

In this contest of one-upmanship, science was sidelined. And in this lay the seeds of the demise of lunar exploration.

★ ★ ★ ★ ★

Two members of the Apollo 11 crew, along with a technician, cross the walkway to board the command module.

BEATING THE SOVIETS

On 16 July 1969, three astronauts lay strapped in their space module atop a massive *Saturn V* rocket. Neil A. Armstrong, Edwin 'Buzz' Aldrin Jr and Michael Collins were the finest products of the National Aeronautics and Space Administration (NASA) and, like the pioneers of the Age of Exploration, they were going on a journey into the unknown.

The mighty US Apollo space program had begun just eight years before, in April of 1961. On the twelfth day of that month, the Russian cosmonaut Yuri Gagarin had become the first person to travel into space and orbit Earth. This had stirred US President John Fitzgerald Kennedy's strong competitive streak.

'I BELIEVE THIS NATION SHOULD COMMIT ITSELF TO ACHIEVING THE GOAL, BEFORE THIS DECADE IS OUT, OF LANDING A MAN ON THE MOON AND RETURNING HIM SAFELY TO EARTH.'

At the time, the American space program was not far behind the Russians in its ability to launch a man into space — on 5 May 1961 Alan Shepard became the first American to orbit the Earth. It lagged, though, in developing the technology to reach the Moon. The Russians had succeeded in launching at least three so-called hard-landing rockets (unmanned spacecraft whose goal was simply hitting the Moon). But buoyed by Shepard's triumph, Kennedy issued a famous challenge when addressing Congress that summer: 'I believe this nation should commit itself to achieving the goal, before this decade is out, of landing a man on the Moon and returning him safely to Earth.'

★★★★★

HEADING INTO ORBIT

With a mighty roar *Apollo 11* lifted off into space, thrilling the million people gathered on the beaches around Kennedy Space Center near Cape Canaveral, Florida. Only eleven minutes after blast-off, it was in orbit with the three astronauts aboard beginning to feel the sensations of weightlessness.

They were used to it. Neil Armstrong, the commander of the mission, was thirty-eight years old, a veteran of seventy-eight combat missions during the Korean War, a test pilot of some of America's most advanced rocket aeroplanes, and a veteran of an earlier Gemini space flight. Armstrong had been selected to become the first man to walk on the Moon.

Thirty-nine-year-old Buzz Aldrin would be Armstrong's partner on the Moon landing. He, too, had been a Korean War fighter pilot and was a Gemini veteran. Aldrin would pilot the lunar module, *Eagle*, which would separate from the command module, *Columbia*, once in the Moon's orbit and bring the two astronauts down to the surface of the Moon.

The third man was Michael Collins, thirty-eight years old, pilot of *Apollo 11* and the *Columbia* command module. Another Gemini veteran, Collins would not get a chance to touch the Moon's surface but had the essential job of making sure the *Eagle* was launched correctly and ensuring that it re-docked safely for its journey back to Earth.

★ ★ ★ ★ ★

A TURBULENT DECADE

While only eight years had passed since Kennedy's challenge, they had been tumultuous ones. Kennedy was dead of an assassin's bullet, as was his brother, Robert. The war in Vietnam had torn the United States apart, America was split by racial divisions and, in some places, crushed by poverty.

Therefore, while there were millions who watched the journey of *Apollo 11* with admiring eyes, there were others who felt differently. To them, space exploration resembled a costly vanity project, meant to enhance the image of the United States abroad while ten million people lived below the poverty line at home.

But nothing would deter NASA from attempting to reach its goal — even in 1967 when tragedy struck and three astronauts on *Apollo 1* died in a fire on the launching pad. (This first manned launch was intended merely to test systems by sending the men into Earth's orbit.) By July 1969, however, Apollo had made four successful manned flights, which had put spacecraft in orbit around the Moon and tested the lunar module.

Unfortunately for the Russians, at this crucial stage one of their chief scientists died and their N1 rocket exploded at least four times during top-secret launch attempts. The Soviet program quickly unravelled.

Now, on 16 July 1969, the United States was about to publicly claim its prize.

★ ★ ★ ★ ★

'YOU CATS TAKE IT EASY'

It took the astronauts three days to reach the Moon. On 19 July, they passed behind the Moon and, while on its 'dark' side, initiated rocket burns that slowed the spacecraft down and corrected its course. It could now enter lunar orbit, about 100 kilometres above the surface of the Moon. Armstrong and Aldrin then entered the *Eagle*, and, on 20 July, separated from *Columbia*. 'You cats take it easy on the lunar surface', Collins told them, his light-hearted comment no doubt masking a real concern.

After it coasted down to an altitude of 6400 metres, the *Eagle* began its powered descent. The surface of the Moon began to appear, pocked with deep craters and with boulder fields scattered across it. Eventually, the *Eagle* was brought by computer into a deep crater, about 200 metres in diameter, called West Crater.

Contending with lunar gravity, and dust blown by the *Eagle*'s rockets, Aldrin and Armstrong could not be entirely sure

Neil Armstrong took this photograph of Buzz Aldrin carrying out scientific tasks on the surface of the Moon.

they had landed, until a contact light lit up on one of the *Eagle*'s landing pads. 'Houston, Tranquility Base here', Armstrong reported. 'The *Eagle* has landed.' There was pandemonium in Mission Control in Houston — joyous celebrations, hugging and kissing, and lighting up of cigars. It was 4.18 pm, US Eastern Daylight Time, on 20 July 1969.

★ ★ ★ ★ ★

'ONE SMALL STEP'

The *Eagle*'s cameras sent back ghostly, almost surreal images of a moonscape that was stark and lifeless. At 10.40 pm, after resting, Armstrong put on his backpack with its portable oxygen system and began climbing down a nine-rung ladder to the surface. Then his left foot touched the ground. 'That's one small step for man, one giant leap for mankind.'

This utterance, heard through hissing static, immediately became famous around the world. But Armstrong always insisted, with irritation, that he had said 'one small step for *a* man', and so his words were officially changed to this, although the recording does not reflect it. Whatever he said, Armstrong — a man of few words — had made history. Around the world people watched in astonishment. It was hard not to feel that something had changed irrevocably in the universe.

★ ★ ★ ★ ★

MEN FROM PLANET EARTH

Soon after, it was Aldrin's turn to climb down to the Moon's surface. The two men then began their scientific tasks: taking soil and rock samples, and capturing solar wind particles. They also set up seismic equipment and a laser mirror that would reflect back a laser beam sent by an observatory telescope in California.

The astronauts planted an American flag and placed a stainless-steel plaque that read: 'Here men from the planet Earth first set foot upon the Moon. July 1969 AD.' It was inscribed with the names of the three astronauts and President Richard Nixon.

After over two hours on the surface of the Moon, Aldrin and Armstrong returned to the *Eagle*. Twelve hours later, Aldrin fired the *Eagle*'s ascent engine and the craft climbed into the sky, where it rendezvoused with the *Columbia*, piloted by Michael Collins. Then all three astronauts flew home.

ALL A HOAX?

Predictably, conspiracy theorists maintained the Moon landing never happened, that the whole thing was staged to distract Americans from the war in Vietnam, or to gain Cold War prestige over the Russians. They pointed out several facets of the landings that they found suspicious. The images broadcast back from the Moon had a surreal quality. The men bouncing around the Moon's surface — unrecognisable in their heavy suits and tinted helmets — could have been almost anyone. And how could Armstrong's first step be filmed when there was no one outside to film it? And, further, how could the American flag flutter at the end of its pole when there was no air?

The answer to the first question was that when he was halfway down the ladder, Armstrong pulled open an outer compartment on the *Eagle* and activated a television camera that had been set up to film his first step onto the Moon.

And the fluttering flag didn't really flutter. It had been packed in a tight roll and, due to the lack of air and gravity, the wrinkles simply took a long time to smooth out.

On 13 August 1969, New York City welcomed the Apollo 11 *crew in a shower of ticker tape. The men had just been released from three weeks in quarantine.*

After splashing down in the Pacific Ocean on 24 July 1969, Collins, Aldrin and Armstrong were placed in quarantine for three weeks, just in case they had brought unknown microorganisms back from the Moon with them. They re-emerged to fame and adulation.

★ ★ ★ ★ ★

THE END OF APOLLO

Most people assumed the success of *Apollo 11* would pave the way for not only more trips to the Moon but also manned voyages to other planets. As it turned out, there were four more manned missions to the Moon, including one, in 1971, in which America's premier astronaut Alan Shepard famously hit a few golf balls. But following the return to Earth of *Apollo 17*, on 19 December 1972, the program was scrapped.

A telling fact about that last mission was that it was the only one whose crew included a real scientist, geologist Harrison Schmitt. The program had been driven by political ambition — the desire of an American president to beat a rival. It had never really become the scientific fact-gathering program it ought to have been.

The public's attention span, never long, soon shifted in other directions. Moon walks became old hat. Moreover, as the 1970s and recession set in, there was no longer the money to fund this incredibly expensive program. And with the Russians having fallen out of the race, there was a growing sense that the Americans had nothing more to prove.

Human beings have not been to the Moon since 1972, and the beautiful orb in the sky has returned to the world of our imaginings, only a little marred by a stainless-steel plaque and one or two golf balls. It seems only fitting.

THE **FALL** OF THE BERLIN WALL

[1989]

★ ★ ★ ★ ★ ★ ★ ★ ★ ★ ★ ★ ★ ★

The symbol of a divided Europe is demolished, bringing an end to the Cold War and reuniting Germany

People gather at the Brandenburg Gate to celebrate the fall of the Berlin Wall. Between 1961 and 1989, both East and West Berliners were denied access to this famous landmark.

Most famous walls in history — the Great Wall of China, Hadrian's Wall, the walls of Troy, to name a few — were constructed to keep people out: Mongols, barbarians, Greeks, whoever. However, the purpose of the Berlin Wall, built in 1961, was the exact opposite: to keep people in.

Specifically, the wall was designed to prevent the people living in the eastern half of Berlin from leaving for the western, democratic, 'free' half of the city. Since the World War II, East Berlin had been part of the Communist German Democratic Republic (GDR). West Berlin was then part of West Germany, or the Federal Republic of Germany.

During the twenty-eight years that it stood, the wall symbolised loss of freedom and the harsh punishment inflicted on those who sought to challenge this loss. Two hundred died attempting to cross to the west. When the nightmare of the Berlin Wall came to an end, it was accompanied by one of the most joyous celebrations of freedom the world has ever witnessed.

★ ★ ★ ★ ★

LIVING IN A DIVIDED CITY

After the end of World War II, Berliners became used to living in a divided city. The victorious Allies divided Germany into four zones, one each for the Americans, British, French and Soviets. Although Berlin lay inside the zone belonging to the Soviets, the city was also divided into four sectors, so that the victorious powers could govern the country jointly from the capital.

But the beginnings of the Cold War interfered with this set-up. In 1948, the three Western powers merged their German zones into one, creating, in 1949, West Germany. In response, the Soviet zone became East Germany. When West Berlin in turn became a part of West Germany, it became an island of Western control at the heart of a communist state.

Berliners made the best of the situation, making shopping trips back and forth, and visiting relatives. Everyone needed to carry identity cards and the checkpoints were a nuisance, but those who had lived through World War II had lived through far, far worse.

★ ★ ★ ★ ★

THE TRAP IS SPRUNG

At about midnight on Saturday 12 August 1961, the S-Bahn trains travelling from East Berlin to West Berlin simply stopped running. Any East Berliners trying to get over to the West were firmly turned away by the East German border guards. East Berliners who happened to be in the West at that point realised that they had to make a daunting decision: they could return — to family and friends — but never cross into the West again; or they could start a new life, alone.

Meanwhile, the streets along the border filled with troop carriers, armoured cars and Soviet tanks. Then trucks arrived, carrying pneumatic drills, barbed wire and concrete posts. In an obviously carefully planned operation, GDR troops began tearing up the pavement just inside the East German border, sinking the posts, stabilising them with poured concrete and stringing barbed wire between them.

The people of East Berlin quickly realised they were completely cut off from the West. The 60,000 East Berliners who worked in the West could no longer reach their jobs. The 'iron curtain' (a term Winston Churchill used to describe the division between communist nations and the West) had become reality.

★ ★ ★ ★ ★

Soviet-controlled German police make a close check of a German truck bound for the British sector of Berlin.

HOW THE OTHER HALF LIVES

During the 1950s, it became clear that the city's Western half had a far better standard of living. With the help of American aid, West Germany had risen from the ashes of World War II. By 1960, West Berlin had built luxury hotels, museums, galleries and concert halls, and publicly celebrated its 100,000th new apartment. Numerous industrial plants — many destroyed during the war — resumed production.

In East Berlin and the GDR, the economy was stagnant. Basic human needs — food and clothing — were sometimes barely met. The ruins of buildings bombed by the Allies during the war remained as a stark reminder of the city's failure to advance. Little wonder then that during the 1950s a total of two

SYMBOLS OF OPPRESSION

One of the wall's earliest victims was an eighteen-year-old construction worker named Peter Fechter. Attempting to climb the wall in 1962, he was shot by the Vopos and fell to the ground on the Eastern side, though within sight of passers-by in the West. As locals and journalists looked on, unable to help, he slowly bled to death.

The last of the almost 200 people killed by the Vopos while attempting to climb or otherwise subvert the wall was twenty-year-old Chris Gueffroy. On 5 February 1989, just a few short months before the wall would come tumbling down, Gueffroy, along with a friend, Christian Gaudian, tried to climb the barrier. He nearly got to the top before being shot through the heart. Gaudian was wounded and sentenced to prison for the attempt, although he was soon released and turned over to the West Berlin government.

There are now memorials to both men in Berlin.

and a half million East Germans fled to the West. One million of these refugees escaped through East Berlin, where there were no walls or barbed wire.

It became clear that if this situation continued, East Berlin would be almost entirely drained of workers, and the claim that the GDR was a happy socialist state would be proved a sham. So Walter Ulbricht, Chairman of the Council of State of the GDR, and his boss in all but name, Soviet Premier Nikita Khrushchev, decided to build themselves a wall.

★ ★ ★ ★ ★

WORK IN PROGRESS

The Berlin Wall was a work in progress that the GDR sought constantly to perfect. At first, it was just barbed wire. Over months, the barbed wire gave way to a concrete-slab wall 4 metres high. Soon this barrier extended for nearly 160 kilometres, completely encircling West Berlin. (Forty-five kilometres of the wall were directly between East and West Berlin.)

Only eight crossing points were left — one specifically for the transfer of deceased persons to relatives in the other half of the city. Another crossing — in the middle of the broad and busy Friedrichstrasse — became famous as 'Checkpoint Charlie', where spies were exchanged, East meeting West with an air of steely tension.

★ ★ ★ ★ ★

RUSH FOR FREEDOM

At first, when the barrier was mere barbed wire and gaps still existed, frantic East Berliners escaped in droves — almost 50,000 in that first month of August 1961 alone. They slipped through the wire at night, swam across canals, sneaked across the boundary clinging to the undercarriages of cars. But then the local guards, some of whom turned a blind eye to such escapes, were replaced by guards from other parts of the country, who had no ties to the city. These men, the Volkspolizei or 'Vopos', were ordered to shoot escapees on sight. Sixteen had died by the end of the year.

Several deaths were witnessed by helpless Western authorities, even the media, and became notorious symbols of the suffering caused by the wall. The wall would give US presidents, from John F. Kennedy to Ronald Reagan, a perfect symbol of a dictatorial communist regime.

★ ★ ★ ★ ★

COMMUNISM RESTRUCTURED

In June of 1985, twenty-four years after the construction of the wall, Soviet President Mikhail Gorbachev introduced reforms under the heading of *perestroika*, or 'restructuring'. The reforms were designed to assist the ailing Soviet economy, and included the introduction of private ownership of businesses and the expansion of foreign trade. Other indications of a loosening of iron government control soon became evident across the Soviet Union. Soon it became much easier for any East German to escape to the West: he or she needed simply to get to Hungary.

Meanwhile, in East Berlin, Erich Honecker, who headed the East German Socialist Party, decried *perestroika* and promised that nothing of the sort would take place in East Germany. But Honecker and his fellow ageing politicians were soon being left behind by a new reality. Gorbachev had heralded a new era of détente, where major powers worked together to defuse international tensions. There would be no need for an armed line between the two Germanys — and no need for a wall.

★ ★ ★ ★ ★

THE WALL COMES DOWN

In the autumn of 1989, thousands of demonstrators marched the streets of East Berlin — an unheard of sign of independence among the citizenry — demanding 'Wir wollen raus', or 'We want to leave'. Finally, on 18 October, Honecker, lacking support both within and outside East Germany, resigned, citing health reasons.

As more and more East Germans streamed to recently liberalised countries of the Soviet Union, such as Hungary and Czechoslovakia, the governments of these countries pleaded with East Germany to do something about the flow of refugees.

On 9 November, the East Berlin Minister of Propaganda, Günter Schabowski, addressed a press conference. In an almost offhand way, he said that people would now be able to cross between the two Germanys whenever they wanted and not have to go through any other countries. When asked when this would take place, Schabowski said: 'As far as I know, effective immediately, right now.'

IN AN ALMOST OFFHAND WAY, HE SAID THAT PEOPLE WOULD NOW BE ABLE TO CROSS BETWEEN THE TWO GERMANYS WHENEVER THEY WANTED AND NOT HAVE TO GO THROUGH ANY OTHER COUNTRIES.

Schabowski's announcement was carried live by radio and television at about 7 pm. Within twenty minutes, thousands of East Berliners had flocked to checkpoints, demanding to be let through to West Berlin. At first, the Vopos attempted to turn them back but, finally, they gave up, opened the gates, and a mass of humanity swarmed through.

Two young boys watch as an East German construction crew, guarded by soldiers, reinforces the newly built Berlin Wall.

There followed one incredible party, carried live on television around the world, as mobs of people, waving bottles of wine and beer, cheering and hugging and kissing, thronged the wall. Hundreds of revellers danced on top of the wall, the most hated symbol of oppression in postwar Berlin history.

The party lasted for weeks. People chipped away at the wall with hammers and pickaxes, taking away chunks of it for souvenirs. In 1990, heavy equipment was brought in to tear down the rest. The only portions of the wall left now are parts of memorials and a section in a Cold War museum.

GERMANY REUNITED

German reunification was officially declared on 3 October 1990.

Since reunification, the road has been a rocky one for East Germany — in part, because the communist states had fallen a long way behind the West economically. Some economists estimate that they still need another twenty years to catch up. Though Germany is one of Europe's leading powers, its recent economic growth has been hampered by reunification, and unemployment remains at high levels in the former East Germany. For some, the shadow of the Wall remains.

9/11
[2001]

★ ★ ★ ★ ★ ★ ★ ★ ★ ★ ★ ★ ★

The attacks that traumatised America, stunned the world and launched a global war on terror

They were four energetic and intense young men. Three of them had studied city planning and engineering. All were well travelled, not only in their native Middle East but also throughout Europe and the United States, where all four, on temporary work visas, took pilot-training lessons. During the last days of their lives, they acted like anyone else might do in America — drawing cash from ATMs, eating at fast-food places, even having a few drinks at a bar. They might easily have been taken for recent immigrants, young professionals enjoying a new lifestyle and looking forward to a bright future in their adopted country.

But they were anything but. For on September 11 2001, Mohammed Atta, Marwan al-Shehhi, Ziad Jarrah and Hani Hanjour would lead fifteen other men onto four passenger planes. Turning these jets into deadly weapons, they would inflict the most devastating terrorist attack in history on the United States, in the name of an Islamic *jihad*, or holy war.

The devastating attacks on the World Trade Center were witnessed on television by millions around the world.

★ ★ ★ ★ ★

PRIME TARGET

By the end of the twentieth century, the United States had become a prime target for Islamic terrorists, due to its long-term support of Israel and of Saudi Arabia. It had supplied both countries with funds, military equipment and training. Chief among its opponents was Al-Qaeda, an Islamic militant group, led by Osama bin Laden. Its goal is to install fundamentalist regimes in all Muslim countries and eradicate all foreign, non-Muslim influence from those nations.

The first attack on US soil was the 1993 bombing of the World Trade Center. Though it caused some damage it failed due to bungles by the terrorists, most of whom were caught and jailed. In 1994, a plot to blow up thirteen American passenger jets was foiled. The following year, terrorists attacked a US military base in Riyadh, Saudi Arabia, killing nineteen American servicemen. The US embassies in Kenya and Tanzania were bombed in 1998, with a total loss of 260 lives; and in October of 2000 seventeen American sailors were killed when a motorboat filled with explosives was ignited next to the US destroyer *Cole*, in the port of Aden in Yemen.

Al-Qaeda learned from these successes and failures. From its headquarters in Afghanistan — then ruled by the Islamic fundamentalist Taliban regime — the group began planning a grand attack on the United States.

★ ★ ★ ★ ★

TRIAL RUNS

The four pilots had been in America for some time, perhaps from as early as January 2000. In early 2001, Osama bin Laden met with subordinates in Afghanistan in order to pick what the 9/11 Commission later referred to as 'the muscle'. These men would be the hijackers who would subdue and threaten the passengers while the trained pilots flew the planes.

After undergoing basic training in Afghanistan, these men began arriving in pairs in the United States in April 2001. During the summer of 2001, the pilots took cross-country reconnaissance flights, carrying knives through airport security and, once on a plane, watching to see when the cockpit doors would be opened.

In June of 2001, the hijackers received final word from bin Laden regarding their targets. They were to be the World Trade Center in New York, the Pentagon in Virginia, and either the White House or the Capitol Building in Washington DC — the nation's headquarters of finance, defence and government.

★ ★ ★ ★ ★

A BEAUTIFUL DAY FOR FLYING

Up and down the eastern seaboard of the United States on September 11, people waking up and getting ready for work remarked on what an extraordinarily beautiful day it was. The sky was clear, the air nearly translucent and the temperature mild, almost balmy. It was a beautiful day for flying.

Al-Qaeda leader Osama bin Laden in Afghanistan in about 1998. Since 9/11, there have been conflicting reports of his death. He is yet to be located.

In less than an hour, four flights carrying hijackers would take off from airports in Boston and Washington. The flights had been chosen with great care. Each was bound for the West Coast, which meant that the planes would have plenty of fuel.

THE TWENTIETH HIJACKER?

The United States missed its greatest chance to stop the 9/11 attacks when it failed to make the most of the arrest of Zacarias Moussaoui, a French citizen of Moroccan descent, who may have been the twentieth hijacker. Moussaoui showed up at the Pan Am International Flight Academy in Eagan, Minnesota, on 13 August 2001, and paid nearly US$7000 in cash to receive training on a Boeing 747 flight simulator. Instructors became suspicious when it became apparent that Moussaoui, whose English was poor, knew little or nothing about flying and was mainly interested in take-offs and landings. They alerted the FBI, who arrested Moussaoui on an immigration violation. The FBI then tried but failed several times to get a warrant to open Moussaoui's laptop — it was considered that they had insufficient evidence to ask for one. Had they been able to do so, they would have found evidence connecting Moussaoui to the 9/11 plotters.

We may never know exactly what Moussaoui's role in 9/11 was. In 2006, he was convicted of conspiring to hijack planes and crash them into the World Trade Center, and sentenced to life imprisonment. But during the trial he wavered between admitting his role, claiming that he was part of another planned terrorist attack, and denying everything. US government officials believe that Moussaoui may have been training as a last-minute replacement for Ziad Jarrah, who, in the summer of 2001, was having second thoughts about his involvement.

The aeroplanes were Boeing 757s or 767s, simulators of which the pilots had trained in.

The terrorists took their first-class seats, in most cases two at the back of the first-class section and two at the front. Then they waited.

★ ★ ★ ★ ★

FLIGHT 11

At 8.14 am, American Airlines Flight 11 out of Boston reached 7600 metres. By 8.25, two attendants on the flight, Betty Ong and Amy Sweeney, were making cell phone calls to American Airlines offices. Ong reported: 'The cockpit is not answering … somebody is stabbed in business class. I think … we're getting hijacked.'

Most likely, the muscle men had risen up as soon as the cockpit door was opened. Two of the unarmed flight attendants were stabbed and then the pilots were killed or incapacitated, and Atta took over the controls. The plane executed a sweeping turn and headed south, down the Hudson River. Betty Ong reported that the plane was flying 'erratically'.

At 8.29 am, air traffic control notified the Federal Aviation Administration that a hijacking had occurred. But it was too late for military aircraft to intercept. Flight 11, swooping down to 300 metres, was speeding over Manhattan Island at 725 kilometres per hour. Flight attendant Sweeney, cried out on her mobile phone: 'We are flying low. We are flying very, very low. We are flying way too low … Oh my God we are way too low.'

Then the phone went dead as American Airlines Flight 11 crashed into the north tower of the World Trade Center, tipping its wings at the last second to create maximum damage to the structure. The exact time was 8:46:40.

★ ★ ★ ★ ★

FLIGHT 175

United Airlines Flight 175 had also taken off from Boston's Logan airport. Before long it stopped responding to enquiries from air traffic control. At 8.51 am, the flight left its normal altitude and also began flying erratically.

As with Flight 11, passengers made panicked calls on their mobile phones. One man, Peter Hanson, called his father to say, 'I think they've taken over the cockpit ... the plane is making strange moves.' A flight attendant reported that both pilots were dead.

THE HIJACKER PILOT PUSHED THE THROTTLES TO FULL POWER AS THE PLANE DIVED DOWN INTO ARLINGTON, VIRGINIA, ACROSS THE POTOMAC RIVER FROM WASHINGTON DC.

At nine o'clock, Peter Hanson called his father again. 'It's getting very bad on the plane', he said. 'Passengers are throwing up and getting sick. The plane is making jerky movements ... I don't think the pilot is flying the plane ... I think we are going down ... Don't worry, Dad: if it happens, it'll be very fast — my God, my God.'

Flight 175 crashed into the south tower of the World Trade Center at 9:03:11.

FLIGHT 77

At 8.46 am, American Airlines Flight 77 reached its cruising altitude of 10,700 metres. At around 9.16, one of the passengers, Barbara Olson, wife of Theodore Olson, the US Solicitor-General, called her husband to say that the plane had been hijacked. At about 9.30, Flight 77 turned, descending to 670 metres. The hijacker pilot pushed the throttles to full power as the plane dived down into Arlington, Virginia, across the Potomac River from Washington DC. When it hit the Pentagon, at 9:37:46, Flight 77 was travelling at more than 850 kilometres per hour.

★ ★ ★ ★ ★

FLIGHT 93

The last of the aeroplanes hijacked that day, United Airlines Flight 93, finally took off at 8.42. It became the only flight where passengers had full knowledge of what had occurred previously — and time in which to attempt to do something about it.

At 9.26, the pilot received the warning from air traffic control to beware of any 'cockpit intrusions', along with the news that two planes had hit the World Trade Center. Soon after, the plane suddenly dropped altitude and the pilot sent out a Mayday distress call. Air traffic control in Cleveland heard the pilot crying, 'Hey, get out of here!' The plane then turned back east.

From mobile phone conversations, the passengers soon knew that it was only a matter of time before the plane would be crashed into a building.

One caller told his wife that they had voted to rush the hijackers. At 9.57, the passengers began their assault, the sounds of which were recorded on the cockpit voice recorder.

A passenger is heard to yell, 'In the cockpit. If we don't, we die.' There are further sounds of commotion and then Jarrah yells: 'Allah is the greatest!'

At 10.03, the aeroplane crashed at a speed in excess of 800 kilometres per hour into a wooded area in Pennsylvania, about twenty minutes' flying time from Washington. Because of the efforts of the passengers, either the Capitol Building or the White House was saved.

★ ★ ★ ★ ★

THE WAR ON TERROR

The 9/11 attacks took the lives of 2749 people in the World Trade Center, 125 at the Pentagon, and 256 on the four planes. It was the worst-ever attack on the United States in its history. The attacks were witnessed on television by millions around the world.

The reaction of the United States was swift. Based on evidence that Al-Qaeda and Osama bin Laden were operating in Afghanistan, President George W. Bush ordered an attack on that country which began on 7 October 2001. Though it displaced the Taliban, it did not discover the whereabouts of Osama bin Laden. In 2003, the United States and Britain also launched an invasion of Iraq, claiming that Saddam Hussein had links to Al-Qaeda (a claim since hotly disputed), sparking a long, bloody and divisive conflict in that country.

Around the world, nations tightened up security in airports, along borders and on public transport. This in turn gave rise to a debate about how to balance security and civil liberties, a debate that still rages as new terrorist attacks take place and new plots are uncovered.

The shock waves from 9/11 are still reverberating around the world. They will do so for decades to come.

This memorial in Union Square, New York City, was one of many impromptu memorials to the victims set up in response to the attack.

BIBLIOGRAPHY

Ambrose, Stephen E. *D-Day: June 6, 1944: The Climactic Battle of World War II*. New York: Simon & Schuster, 1994.

Black, Jeremy. *The Seventy Great Battles in History*. London, Thames & Hudson, 2005.

Bobrick, Benson. *Angel in the Whirlwind: The Triumph of the American Revolution*. New York: Simon & Schuster, 1997.

Bradford, Ernle. *Julius Caesar: The Pursuit of Power*. New York: William Morrow & Co., 1984.

Cantor, Norman F. *In the Wake of the Plague: The Black Death and the World It Made*. New York: The Free Press, 2001.

Collins, Michael. *Liftoff: The Story of Americaís Adventure in Space*. New York: Grove Press, 1988.

Crankshaw, Edward. *The Shadow of the Winter Palace: Russia's Drift to Revolution 1825–1917*. New York: Viking Press, 1976.

Der Spiegel Magazine: *Reporters, Writers and Editors. Inside 9-11: What Really Happened*. New York: St Martinís Press, 2001.

Devries, Kelly. *The Battles of the Medieval World: From Hastings to Constantinople*. New York: Barnes & Noble, 2006.

Dwyer, Jim and Kevin Flynn. *102 Minutes: The Untold Story of the Fight to Survive inside the Twin Towers*. New York: Times Books, 2005.

Foster, R.F. *Modern Ireland: 1600–1972*. London: Penguin, 1988.

Gardner, Brian. *The Big Push: A Portrait of the Battle of the Somme*. New York: William Morrow, 1963.

Herlihy, David. *The Black Death and the Transformation of the West*. Cambridge, Massachusetts: Harvard University Press, 1997.

Hibbert, Christopher. *The Days of the French Revolution*. New York: William Morrow & Co., 1980.

Howarth, David. *Waterloo: Day of Battle*. New York: Atheneum, 1968.

Kelly, John. *The Great Mortality: An Intimate History of the Black Death, the Most Devastating Plague of All Time*. New York: HarperCollins, 2005.

Kohn, George Childs. *Dictionary of Wars*. New York: Checkmark Books, 2007.

Lewis, Richard S. *The Voyages of Apollo: The Exploration of the Moon*. New York: The New York Times Book Co., 1974.

Lloyd, Alan. *The Spanish Century: A Narrative History of Spain from Ferdinand and Isabella to Franco*. Garden City: Doubleday & Co., 1964.

Lucie-Smith, Edward A. *Joan of Arc*. New York: W.W. Norton & Co., 1976.

McCourt, Malachy. *History of Ireland*. Philadelphia: Running Press, 2004.

Madden, Thomas F. *Crusades: The Illustrated History*. Ann Arbor: University of Michigan Press, 2004.

Martin, Colin and Geoffrey Parker. *The Spanish Armada*. New York: W.W. Norton & Co., 1988.

Mattingly, Garrett. *The Armada*. Boston: Houghton, Mifflin Company, 1959.

Moorehead, Alan. *Gallipoli*. New York: Harper & Brothers, 1956.

Parenti, Michael. *The Assassination of Julius Caesar: A People's History of Ancient Rome*. New York, London: The New Press, 2003.

Pernoud, Régine. *The Retrial of Joan of Arc: The Evidence at the Trial for Her Rehabilitation, 1450–1456*. New York: Harcourt, Brace & Co., 1955.

Posner, Gerald. *Case Closed: Lee Harvey Oswald and the Assassination of JFK*. New York: Random House, 1993.

Read, Anthony and David Fisher. *Berlin Rising: Biography of a City*. New York: W.W. Norton & Co., 1994.

Reston, James Jr. *Dogs of God: Columbus, the Inquisition, and the Defeat of the Moors*. New York: Doubleday, 2005.

Salisbury, Harrison E. *Russia in Revolution: 1900–1930*. New York: Holt, Rinehart & Winston, 1978.

Schama, Simon. *Citizens: A Chronicle of the French Revolution*. New York: Alfred A. Knopf, 1989.

Thompson, Josiah. *Six Seconds in Dallas: A Micro-Study of the Kennedy Assassination*. New York: Random House, 1967.

Turner, John Frayn. *Invasion, í44: The Story of D-Day in Normandy*. New York: G.P. Putnamís Sons, 1959.

Ward-Perkins, Bryan. *The Fall of Rome and the End of Civilization*. Oxford: Oxford University Press, 2005.

Weintraub, Stanley. *Long Day's Journey into War: December 7, 1941*. New York: Dutton, 1991.

Wilford, John Noble. *The Mysterious Story of Columbus: An Exploration of the Myth, the Man, the Legacy*. New York: Alfred A. Knopf, 1991.

Wyden, Peter. *Day One: Before Hiroshima and After*. New York: Simon & Schuster, 1984.

ABOUT THE AUTHOR

Joseph Cummins is the author of *History's Great Untold Stories*, *History's Greatest Hits*, *Turn Around and Run Like Hell*, *Great Rivals in History*, *Cast Away*, *First Encounters* and *Eaten by a Giant Clam* for Murdoch Books, as well as *Anything for a Vote: A History of Dirty Tricks* and *October Surprises in America's Presidential Elections* (Quirk). He has also edited two anthologies for Lyons Press, *Cannibals: Shocking True Stories of the Last Taboo on Land and at Sea* (2002) and *The Greatest Search and Rescue Stories Ever Told* (2001), and written a novel called *The Show Train* (Akashic Books, 2001). He lives in Maplewood, New Jersey.

INDEX

Published in 2010 by Pier 9, an imprint of Murdoch Books Pty Limited

Murdoch Books Australia
Pier 8/9
23 Hickson Road
Millers Point NSW 2000
Phone: +61 (0) 2 8220 2000
Fax: +61 (0) 2 8220 2558
www.murdochbooks.com.au

Murdoch Books UK Limited
Erico House, 6th Floor
93–99 Upper Richmond Road
Putney, London SW15 2TG
Phone: +44 (0) 20 8785 5995
Fax: +44 (0) 20 8785 5985
www.murdochbooks.co.uk

Publisher: Diana Hill
Project Editor: Emma Hutchinson
Copy Editors: Scott Forbes and Diane Furness
Designer: Hugh Ford

Picture Sources:
Corbis: back cover (top middle, bottom left and middle), pages 2–3, 26, 35, 110, 115, 118, 140, 152, 160, 172, 185, 188–189, 202, 206, 209, 231
Getty Images: front cover, pages 82-83, 96-97, 128, 150–151, 155, 166, 170, 182, 194, 199, 204–205, 212–213, 218, 226, 236, 241
Library of Congress: page 143
Photolibrary: back cover (top left and right, bottom right), pages 6, 10–11, 12, 16, 19, 22, 29, 32, 38-39, 42–43, 46, 50–51, 54, 56, 60, 63, 66, 71, 74, 76, 86, 89, 90, 94, 98, 101, 106–107, 120, 123, 130, 135, 138, 162, 174, 180, 223, 228, 238, 246
Picture Desk/The Art Archive: pages 80, 146

National Library of Australia Cataloguing-in-Publication Data
Author: Cummins, Joseph.
Title: The history files: history's greatest hits : famous events we should all know about / Joseph Cummins.
ISBN: 978-1-74196-657-2 (hbk.).
Notes: Includes index. Bibliography.
Subjects: World history.
Dewey Number: 909

A catalogue record for this book is available from the British Library.

PRINTED IN CHINA.